PRAISE FOR WHY IS A VERB

"Butler and Price provide a bold, practical, timely argument why purpose is the key to unlocking our full potential, and they offer a clear and actionable framework for helping teams and individuals achieve their goals."

JESSICA JENSEN, *Chief Marketing Officer*
INDEED

"While the relationship between employee engagement and organizational performance has been well established, many leaders and teams continue to struggle with making it a reality. Why Is a Verb *combines incisive research insight with broad and deep frontline experience to produce the kind of practical, evidence-based approach leaders have been hungering for—one that goes beyond merely articulating purpose to the real work of implementation and measurement."*

DAN WITTERS, *Research Director*
National Health and Well-Being Index,
GALLUP

"Why Is a Verb *captivates from the start, challenging preconceived notions and buzzwords around purpose. In a world filled with empty slogans, this book delves into the process of operationalizing purpose, offering actionable tactics for success. It is a must-read for all who believe in the transformative power of purpose and seek a practical path to turn it into reality."*

JODIE GOULDEN, *Organization Design Expert*
ORGDESIGN WORKS

"Strong management is based on real psychology. Butler and Price rebuild our assumptions about how purpose works based on detailed research, from the science of happiness to behavioral economics, to deliver a powerful, practical program for improving labor productivity."

PATRICIA PHILLIPS, *Chair*
HEADVERSITY

"Organizations of different sizes and sectors have more in common than they realize—especially when it comes to their struggles with WHY. The authors come to the challenge with a rare and potent blend of leadership experience, research chops, and advisory tools. The result is a set of principled recommendations that can work anywhere."

BILL CIPRICK, *Chief Executive Officer*
OPTIMI HEALTH

"Employee engagement is increasingly, and rightly, recognized as a primary driver of performance. While expert insight and success continues to grow in this critical area, many leaders remain hesitant to go 'all-in.' Why Is a Verb *demystifies the moving parts in plain language, backed up by compelling research and keen analysis, and combines them into a holistic program results-oriented leaders will love."*

JEFF TETZ, *Chief Executive Officer*
RESULTS

"When managers appreciate employees and highlight how their contributions fit into the bigger picture, productivity and performance soar. Why Is a Verb *will help you focus on critical, often overlooked steps to put your corporate WHY into practice. It's also a great read."*

TOM SHORT, *Co-founder & Chief Customer Officer*
KUDOS

HOW CAN WHY WORK BETTER?

"I often feel like a musician who can't hear themselves play."

—GEN Z EMPLOYEE

Everyone wants work to matter.

Employees want the joy of having impact.

Leaders want the impact to drive productivity.

Top value creators, from Apple to Tesla, show what can happen when purpose and productivity mesh.

Less clear? How to replicate such success.

Over half a century, experts' preferred practice—publishing purpose or WHY statements—has become a standard ritual among high-aspiration organizations.

Yet something isn't working.

- Less than one in three leaders actually uses these tools.
- Barely one in five employees feels engaged.
- Productivity growth has fallen to historic lows.

This book proposes a bold new approach, the product of a unique five-year quest by two social scientists turned management practitioners. Combining years of field work with research insight, it reveals:

- How humans' distinctive need for purpose has driven our flourishing as a species;
- How the feeling has been dulled by modern work and life;
- How tapping its power means going beyond mere words.

What emerges is a fresh perspective on what purpose-driven leadership really entails: less talking about your company's impact than helping employees feel their own.

STEPHEN BUTLER is a management consultant and globally featured TEDx speaker. KARISSA PRICE is Chief Marketing Officer at Dragonfruit AI and a former Fortune 100 marketing executive.

Since earning social science doctorates at Harvard and Cambridge and starting careers at The Boston Consulting Group, they've created over five decades of value as executives, entrepreneurs, and advisors.

WHY
is a
VERB

How Well-Managed Teams
Turn Purpose
into Productivity

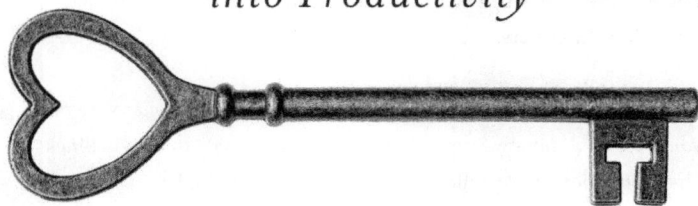

STEPHEN BUTLER, PhD
and KARISSA PRICE, PhD

To our teachers

CONTENTS

"How selfish soever man may be supposed, there are evidently some principles in his nature, which interest him in the fortune of others, and render their happiness necessary to him, though he derives nothing from it except the pleasure of seeing it."

ADAM SMITH
The Theory of Moral Sentiments (1759)

FOREWORD

We Need Purpose to Work

"An idea can only become a reality once it is broken down into organized, actionable elements."

SCOTT BELSKY

SATURDAY, FEBRUARY 1, 2020, Krakow. I was visiting Marriott hotels in Poland when I received a call from our headquarters in Bethesda. Italy, the first European country to place municipalities in COVID-19 lockdown, was reportedly considering locking down its entire northern region. With the virus spreading faster than anticipated, I was advised to cut my trip short. As I boarded a flight out hours later, I experienced mixed emotions:. relief that I was healthy and would soon be reunited with my family; concern about the impact this rapidly growing crisis might have on people everywhere—particularly ours.

At the time, Marriott International had hundreds of thousands of associates in 134 countries. Within months, revenues would drop nearly 90 percent and our stock price by almost two-thirds. Some of our hotels would have to close their doors—unheard of in our ninety-six-year history. Other properties would become dedicated to accommodating frontline workers.

The toughest decisions we faced were the ones that impacted the foundation of Marriott's success: our associates. With demand in free fall, we had to make difficult choices, including furloughing thousands globally. However, even in that darkest hour, we were guided by our people-first culture. We had to support all our people, whether or not we had work for them. We expanded training programs, offered health support, and provided financial assistance. We collaborated with other companies less affected by the pandemic to find work opportunities for our furloughed associates while engaging governments to secure additional relief.

Within a year, demand started to return almost as quickly as it had disappeared. This brought new talent challenges. Job vacancies in the bruised hospitality sector hit an all-time high; one in four new Marriott hires was leaving within ninety days. If we couldn't deliver the service guests expected, we knew much of what we'd worked so hard to bring back might be lost.

We pressed ahead by doubling down on the belief that helped us build the world's largest hospitality company: In the words of our founder, J.W. Marriott, Sr., "If we take care of our associates, they will take care of our guests, and the guests will come back again and again." We recommitted to organizational leadership, promoting a sense of collective responsibility for our success, and leaned into the three "signature elements" of our people strategy: Growing Great Leaders, Investing in Associates, and Access to Opportunity.

As soon as travel bans were lifted, our senior leaders went back out on the road to reengage with the frontline. We reignited initiatives the pandemic had put on hold and launched new programs to support our signature elements. We developed fresh leadership programs, revisited our compensation framework, and amplified our focus on the whole person. Our new people brand, Be™, reinforced our commitment to associates that they can begin their career, belong to an amazing global team, and become the best version of themselves. We also responded to the needs of the post-COVID workforce by increasing flexibility and choice. This enabled us to tap into a broader talent pool of individuals who couldn't contemplate a career in hospitality previously, while increasing retention of those who had been with us for years.

The results of these efforts? Less than three years after the pandemic began, Marriott moved into the top ten spot on the Fortune Best Companies to Work for in 2023, a list it had been on for 26 consecutive years. Ninety-two percent of our associates called our company a "Great Place to Work...where employees trust the people they work for, have pride in what they do, and enjoy the people they work with"—seven points higher than before the pandemic and a full thirty-five points higher than a typical business.

This swift rebound to new heights has prompted outsiders to ask how we did it. The answer lies in our core values, established over nearly a century in business. Through all of Marriott's evolution and growth, we've remained committed to the principles that shape our people-first culture. From our humble beginnings as a nine-seat root beer stand to our current global portfolio of nearly 8,700 properties in 139 countries and territories, we have always been a people business. Marriott's reputation with our customers is driven by the experiences we shape for them. Those expectations define our associates' purpose at work, connecting people through the power of travel, which drives our business success.

This brings us to *Why Is a Verb*. This book tackles a problem many wrestle with: how purpose in the workplace, while celebrated, has a mixed track record when it comes to tangible results. Communicating the WHY is often treated like the main event, with the real work of implementation an afterthought. It is no surprise to hear from Gallup that barely one in five workers worldwide feel engaged at work—or that even fewer say they "live their purpose at work."

Much of Marriott's success flows from appreciating this simple truth: Ideas don't implement themselves; people do. Purpose isn't just words on posters stuck on the walls of a workspace. It's a daily practice, a constant rediscovery that drives superior performance. It's a sense of tenacity and grit that only kicks in once you live it.

As our experience at Marriott attests, WHY can drive real results, and as this book suggests, if it is thoughtfully implemented and authentically lived, it unleashes untapped reserves of energy and creativity, elevating productivity, shareholder value, and fulfillment for everyone involved, from senior leadership to the frontline. Butler and Price offer a practical guide to implementing purpose, drawing on research and experience that shows how an authentic and systematic approach can help it deliver for individuals and organizations alike.

In this changing world, the most constructive way any of us can make a difference, whether working an entry-level job at a start-up or taking an established brand to new heights, may simply be this: Make your work mean something. Take it from a company whose WHY has served it well for almost a century and helped us rise higher through tremendous adversity.

Ty Breland
EVP & Chief Human Resources Officer
Marriott International
Bethesda, February 2024

PREFACE

Making WHY Work

"A man will be imprisoned in a room with a door that's unlocked and opens inwards; as long as it does not occur to him to pull rather than push."

LUDWIG WITTGENSTEIN

A FEW YEARS AGO, THE CEO of a fast-growing consumer packaged goods company called a strategy consultant with an unusual request: She wanted him to run a WHY workshop.

"WowCo" was pivoting its business model, but not everyone was on board. After watching a TED Talk, the CEO decided a new purpose statement might be the flag the company could rally around.

Conditions seemed promising. The team was keen, the advisor an experienced facilitator. To "find their WHY," as the team put it, they just had to follow steps laid out in a best-selling workbook.

What they got instead was disaster.

Participants struggled to articulate their personal WHYs. Teams struggled to find themes. When the full group gathered to craft a company mission, clashing opinions led to what one manager later called "a battle royale."

"Maybe this purpose thing," the CEO sadly confided to the advisor, "is BS."

That night, the consultant tried to figure out what had gone wrong. They'd followed the book to a T. Was the approach perhaps unsuited to earlier stage companies, where culture was less developed? Was the problem that WowCo's managers were mostly engineers, who preferred fact to vision? Or was the new direction, shifting from risky proprietary products to more reliable white-label manufacturing, simply uninspiring?

The next day, he polled his LinkedIn network: Did anyone have experience with corporate purpose exercises?

To his surprise, the first to respond was a former colleague from the global consultancy where he'd started his career, now an executive at one of the world's biggest companies. He was delighted to hear from her but unsure how relevant her experience might be.

They spoke for over two hours. By the time they hung up, the advisor's perspective had shifted.

He started to think the CEO might be right.

THE PARADOX

In 2018, Estée Lauder's newly appointed Chief Sustainability & ESG Officer, Nancy Mahon, told a journalist we were living in "the golden age of purpose."

It isn't hard to appreciate what she meant. Over the last two decades, searches for purpose-related terms have surged tenfold. Talks about WHY have racked up tens of millions of views. Books on the subject have topped bestseller lists. Millennials and Gen Zers rank meaning among their top workplace requirements.

Business leaders have noticed. Companies now invest more than ever in purpose initiatives, from mission and team building exercises, to environmental, social, and governance (ESG) investments, to general corporate citizenship. CEOs talk about their WHYs on analyst calls. The world's biggest investor, BlackRock's Larry Fink, now only invests in companies that make "a positive contribution to society." The US Business Roundtable recently redefined the purpose of its members, for the first time in its fifty-year history, to include stakeholder interests.

Why all this interest in WHY?

When it works, the rewards are great. Purposeful employees live happier, healthier lives, with fewer absences and lower turnover. Purpose-driven companies outperform the market several times over.

But that observation can be misleading, for what counts as purpose-driven is subjective. The top reason CEOs have been willing to invest in business purpose is that it promises to drive a more tangible measure—employee engagement—which they have come to see as the key to value creation's increasingly elusive Holy Grail: labor productivity growth.

From one perspective, efforts to foster the feeling of purpose at work appear to be paying off. Since Gallup began tracking it in 2012, global employee engagement has almost doubled. McKinsey recently found that 85 percent of upper managers feel they can live their purpose in their jobs.

From another, however, they're not.

Global engagement still languishes below one in four. Another workplace study suggests white-collar workers are productive less than three hours a day. That same McKinsey study found that, among the frontline managers and employees who make up most of the workforce, less than one in six feels purposeful.

Bottom line: Our unprecedented interest and investment in WHY is starting to look like a tragic waste.

THE CHALLENGE

How did it happen?

Until half a century ago, if leaders thought about "business purpose," it was to explain why certain expenses were tax deductible.

Then, in the midst of the worst bear market since the Great Depression, the "father of modern management" turned the phrase on its head. Peter Drucker suggested that business purpose should refer not

to activities that serve a business, but to activities a business serves—
and that defining these should be every leader's prime concern.

Drucker's revolutionary spark took the better part of three
decades to catch. By the turn of the century, it had become a wildfire.
Nearly every public company, and private firms that aspired to join
their ranks, published a mission, vision, or values statement—often
all three.

As freshly minted consultants, we found ourselves tasked with
helping Fortune 500 and global equivalent clients craft purpose
statements as a standard part of strategic renewals. Yet relatively little
thought went into the process. For most, purpose was just another
box to check—a wordsmithing exercise some leapt into enthusiasti-
cally while others eyed their watches.

As entrepreneurs and mid-level executives over the next decade
and a half, we became purpose-box checkers ourselves. By the time
we returned to the task as C-suite advisors, the game had changed.
WHY had become a noun, spelled in all caps. The goal had shifted
from mapping a direction to rallying around what was already present. Dedicated purpose experts came in with new, formal methodologies. Staff were consulted. Detailed market research and capability
assessments followed.

Leaders told researchers like Bain & Company, which began
studying the practice in the early 90s, how much they loved their
new, hard-won WHYs. But three things gave us pause.

For starters, staff rarely shared leaders' enthusiasm for corporate
purpose statements, not finding them actionable. Managers rarely called
upon them. Worse, after temporary upticks, employee engagement
and productivity tended to revert to their starting points—often below.

In the wake of the WowCo workshop, and similar experiences
in corporate contexts, we spotted cracks in what had become the
standard approach to business purpose. We were dismayed but not
surprised to learn more than two in three US employees were indif-
ferent to their work, with one in five "actively disengaged."

We thought, "There has to be a better way."

THE ANALYSIS

Ground zero for this project was a pattern we noticed: a difference between the way clients and teams talked about purpose in and outside of WHY workshops.

In them, employees generally accepted "expert" assumptions about how purpose can be turned into action:

- The idea that a personal WHY can be articulated as a rationale for doing what we do for a living;
- The belief that this is a life-defining, if elusive, force formed before we even start our careers;
- The idea that it can be surfaced by reflecting upon our experiences; and
- The notion that we're all articulate enough to synthesize our purpose into a sentence that can guide us for life.

Outside workshops, purpose remained more nebulous. If individuals discussed it at all, it was as vague feelings they could not clearly articulate, beyond a level so generic as to be of limited guidance ("I love helping people"). These feelings tended to change with context—for example, after a change in role or company ownership. All this made us wonder.

- What if the expert assumptions were wrong?
- What if purpose isn't an enduring trait we can find by one-off reflection and then heed for life?
- What if, instead, it's a more dynamic sense of alignment between our evolving selves and our changing environments?

To our surprise, we turned out to be far from alone in suspecting that the standard approach to purpose might be the Emperor's New Clothes: accepted by dint of its popularity, rather than conviction. With hopeful clients and curious colleagues cheering us on, we leaned into our experience as strategists and managers—and, not for the first time in our careers, our doctoral training—in search of something better.

We began by asking why we even feel a need for WHY, starting with the science of well-being, its insights into the emotional needs that shape our behavior, and purpose's apparent biological function.

This led us to the relatively nascent field of evolutionary biology, which seeks to understand modern psychological malaise as the result of naturally helpful inclinations that have outgrown their usefulness.

As historian Yuval Noah Harari notes in his popular *Sapiens: A Brief History of Humankind,* human beings are distinguished as a species by our ability to collaborate in large numbers. This enabled us to progress from about twenty thousand vulnerable individuals a hundred thousand years ago, inhabiting one corner of one continent and surrounded by larger and faster predators and prey, to the planet's preeminent species, a billion strong, before we had electricity.

Anthropologists and biologists have long puzzled over how this remarkable transformation happened. Intelligence can't explain it. Paleontological evidence suggests that our failed hominid rivals like Neanderthals and Homo erectus were also intelligent.

Evolutionary biologists have zeroed in on Homo sapiens's distinctive emotional reward system, which motivated us to collaborate in an unusually dynamic fashion. Over tens of millennia, human individuals appear to have been intrinsically motivated to take on and master specialized roles, from tracker to farmer to explorer, in order to promote their groups' survival. Moreover, we loved adapting those roles as circumstances required. As we multiplied and spread across a warming planet, we developed new skills and passed them down to be further developed.

We manifested an innate need to impact others. A natural drive to specialize, master, and innovate.

To our ears, that sounded a lot like not just belief, according to Harari, but *purpose.*

Maybe, we thought, WHY is not something we've only recently started to care about.

Maybe it's something we're wired for—and have lost.

THE LOSS

Our forays into positive and evolutionary psychology not only began to explain our natural propensity for purpose. It also suggested why many now struggle to experience it.

To identify changes that may have impeded our ability to find meaning, we turned our focus to the history, sociology, and economics of work.

A prime suspect was civilization itself. Feeling our individual impact on a tribe of a hundred was relatively easy. But doing so in communities of thousands, let alone millions? That's much harder.

The way we came to make our living within an artificial type of mini tribe—the company—made things worse.

The real dividing line was the Industrial Revolution. This spurred a value creation miracle: As a species, we've produced more wealth in the last 250 years than in the previous fifty thousand.

Yet technology did not operate itself. The foundation of modern economic practice was our doubling down on the individual specialization required to improve productivity.

Breaking down complex tasks into simpler ones allows today's employees to produce at least twenty times more per hour than our preindustrial ancestors.

This has doubled our lifespans. Increased our numbers eightfold. Lifted a third of the species out of poverty.

Yet it has come at a harrowing psychological cost: distance from the personal impact we experienced in preindustrial cooperation.

Nineteenth-century social observers spotted this alienation on factory floors. In the course of a few generations, it led to ideological division, labor conflict, even war.

Since then, it has become endemic. Today, while 89 percent of companies cite customer experience as a top priority, less than a third of jobs are customer-facing. Most of us are expected to have impact we can't see. To add injury to insult, specialization's economic benefits have tailed off. It's not just shareholders feeling the drag of weak productivity growth. Compounded by rising offshore competition, generations of employees have experienced declining real wage growth. Millennials and Gen Zers have arrived in the workplace with the lowest career expectations in living memory, anticipating a lower standard of living than their parents. While leaders applaud the rise of generative artificial intelligence (AI), on the front line, it's clouding the horizon even further.

The biggest impact of industrialization's stalled miracle may be on those who have yet to feel its upside. Half of the species, four billion people, may be stuck below the global poverty line until companies can find their next gear.

THE SOLUTION

With this perspective in hand, we circled back to our work with teams.

Our objective: To move beyond workshop- and articulation-based approaches to finding WHY, which we found to be better suited to generating hypotheses than delivering results. To identify practices that are more natural, accessible, and replicable: a dynamic take on purpose that can engage managers *and employees*, and raise team productivity in virtually any setting. This meant an approach that would affect more than those in senior roles. More than just sectors with an obvious social impact, like cleantech. More than later-stage companies, where value focus has been largely established. More than just among teams with great managers, largely responsible for the limited engagement we already enjoy.

We sought measures that could work anywhere, sustainably. We observed and tested purpose-fostering techniques with hundreds of individuals and dozens of teams at companies of various sectors, sizes, and geographies, with a view to their impact on two core measures: engagement and productivity.

Our eureka moment came in two parts.

First was in conversation with a CEO who felt the social impact of any firm was best achieved not by "giving back" profits to good causes, but making profits through "healing customers' pain."

The other was a plaintive cry from a Gen Z employee: "I often feel like a musician who can't hear themselves play."

We located managers' purpose role at the intersection of two insights. Like that CEO, the father of modern economics, Adam Smith, believed that human beings' economic, value-creating behavior rested on an essential psychological precondition: our capacity for cognitive empathy, without which we could not imagine what products or services customers might value (chapter 5).*

It seemed no accident that mainstream managers embraced this insight as their interest in purpose exploded in the late twentieth century (chapter 2). It became clear that when we say the purpose of the company is value creation, what we mean is solving human problems (chapter 4). Inspired by Drucker and others, corporations realized they could not build fresh market insight or develop proprietary know-how without engaging their people around appreciating the needs of others, including those they worked with (chapters 1 and 2).

Thus, Key Insight #1:

The essential function of business purpose is the operationalization of empathy, with a view toward maximizing customer value and internal efficiency.

Day by day, this means helping employees feel the rewards of their input and cooperation in the form of better feedback loops, upon which managers can then build, per our Gen Z musician, "amps" that convey their impact on others (chapter 8). Corporate citizenship initiatives may well generate pride and loyalty among employees. What they can't inspire? Productivity. As compellingly argued in Daniel Pink's *Drive: The Surprising Truth About What Motivates Us,* our best efforts in most jobs are propelled by intrinsic reward and the sense that our personal work makes a difference (chapter 2).

Hence, Key Insight #2:

Operationalizing empathy means internalizing individual purpose.

To test these ideas, our clients and teams performed trials of

---

* Cognitive empathy is distinct from what psychologists call "affective empathy," where we actually feel what others feel. The latter is what many now mean by the unmodified term. It is relatively rare, thought to be naturally present in less than a fifth of human beings, and unlearnable. When we use it unmodified here, however, we refer to the more intellectual, learnable skill.

various solutions (chapter 8). Team dashboards. Personal dashboards. Peer recognition systems. Accountability, Resources, and Consequences (ARC) agreements. They also tracked the impact of such tools, from pulse engagement surveys to situation-specific productivity metrics based on what gets measured gets improved.

We drilled down on where purpose implementations go wrong (chapter 8). It became clear they are less addition than multiplication functions. What can look to managers like discrete initiatives—where an 80 percent implementation, say, might be expected to drive 80 percent improvement—form part of a single experience for employees. Ignore a key component and one may as well deliver a car without a key, or worse, raise expectations and fail to match the walk with the talk across the board When this happens engagement tends to go down.

The most common source of such problems? Evaluating managers by financial metrics alone without regard for people results, or measuring the latter without plans to address them by supporting leadership development.*

We discovered the responsibility to address this did not fall entirely on managers. Leveraging purpose also requires a mindset shift among employees, from seeing WHY as a singular lifelong calling to a perpetual, mindful search for "Self-Impact Fit": a match between our energies, skills, and the needs of those we would impact. *If we try to live by a WHY sentence that will serve us for life, we become the ones serving a life sentence.* Better to focus on aligning these moving parts as ongoing exercises, starting with a tool we developed for this purpose: the Self-Impact Compass (chapter 7).

Thus, aligning manager and employee efforts around feeling the impact drives value in three key ways:

1. *It operationalizes empathy and internalizes individual purpose.* Companies create value by collaboratively coming up with new and better solutions to problems. Doing so requires shared

---

* By the time the latter begin to drag on financial performance, long-term damage is often done.

empathy for customers and mutual empathy among teams.

2. *Aligning efforts centered on purpose-feeling helps everyone involved appreciate the intrinsic social value of running a great business, regardless of size or sector (with the exception of those that actively harm customers, like tobacco).* Feeling WHY at work is not just a contribution to individual well-being and company performance. Productivity growth helps customers, communities, and the world (chapter 1).

3. *A more natural and holistic model of purpose can spark a virtuous, self-energizing cycle of individual discovery.* The idea that individuals have only one WHY can be discouraging, especially when it feels too general or temporary. A living, evolving WHY changes this. The ongoing process of discovery (having impact on ourselves) is more energizing, increasing our chances of discovering new aspects of reality that solve problems. Indeed, this is the WHY we all share: the natural human feeling we've lost through economic and social developments.

The good news? The tools we need to make WHY work, from more constructive management techniques to more realistic employee attitudes, are well within reach (chapters 7 and 8). We just need to grasp and run with them.

While these insights may be timeless, acting on them has never been more timely. Favorable trends—from an incoming generation of purpose-oriented managers to less mind-numbing jobs to AI-facilitated impact measurement (chapter 9)—now position us to achieve an outsize surge in productivity and value creation, the likes of which we've not seen for generations. It's no exaggeration to suggest that, within two decades, we may realize the once-incredible dream of Dow 100,000.

For all the misery implied by current engagement and productivity numbers, it would be a mistake to see WHY efforts to date as wasted. As the transformative IBM CEO Thomas J. Watson observed, "failure is a great teacher." The struggles of recent years have shown how much WHY matters to employees, managers, and shareholders; what it can achieve when it works; and how much we have yet to understand. They have positioned us to help purpose finally deliver on its manifold promise. More engaged teams. Revived productivity growth. Greater individual happiness. All of which adds up to realizing the full benefits of industrialization and unprecedented human flourishing.

We may not be living in purpose's golden age. But there's every reason to believe we're standing on its threshold.

SB/KP
San Francisco/Sun Valley
January 2024

KEY TAKEAWAYS 🔑

1. This century has seen businesses and individuals invest unprecedented time and money persuading themselves that their work matters (chapters 1 and 2).

2. Despite these efforts, however, and success in senior ranks, studies suggest less than one in six feels purposeful or engaged at work.

3. The unclear impact of purpose-fostering exercises arise from questionable/unproven assumptions—in particular, that we all have one lifelong WHY that defines us.

4. Evolutionary psychology suggests that human beings' survival advantage came from an innate need for purpose-feeling—a desire to have impact on others by taking on specialized roles, which we then adapted based on our groups' changing needs.

5. Aspects of modern life and work have dulled our purpose-feeling, including the size of our societies and a doubling down on specialization that has driven miraculous, if declining, productivity growth and increased the psychological distance between our work and its impact.

6. We've worked with dozens of teams at companies in various sectors and sizes to find replicable, measurable ways to revive purpose-feeling, engagement, and productivity. Our prescriptions unlock the following three insights:

    a. *Value creation operationalizes empathy* so that teams better understand the needs of their clients and more efficiently align their efforts with that of our colleagues;

    b. *Operationalizing empathy means internalizing purpose* so that individuals feel the impact of their work; and

    c. *WHY may be more constructively seen as a dynamic, lifelong journey of discovery* through which we find a series of "Self-Impact Fits"—not merely a single WHY sentence that we must then harness ourselves to for life.

7. The benefits of a more grounded and practical approach include the following practices, all of which require consistency and comprehensiveness to work:

a. Better alignment of manager and employee efforts around empathy and impact, and, thus, better outcomes;

b. A revival of productivity growth that can extend the benefits of modern economics to more of the species; and

c. Helping individuals feel happier in their lives through a sense of living, durable purpose at work, where the focus is on delight in perpetual discovery, not on harnessing ourselves to one WHY that defines (and confines) us.

8. These techniques, combined with favorable trends, such as more purpose-driven managers and AI-facilitated impact measurement, puts us on the path to a fully-realized Golden Age of Purpose.

Part One: *THE PROBLEM WITH WHY*

"I couldn't stand living in a society that admires the emperor's new clothes, when I see so clearly that he is naked."

PATRICIA MCCONNELL

CHAPTER 1

Our Purpose Paradox

"Every business is full of sh*t. They don't even tell you about the product no more. They just tell you how much charity they do."

CHRIS ROCK

MONTHS BEFORE COVID-19 ARRIVED, a group of almost two hundred CEOs from leading American companies, broke with a half century of tradition to restate its view on the purpose of business.

At its 1972 inception, the Business Roundtable (BRT) had cohered around a principle articulated by economist Milton Friedman two years earlier: "the one and only social responsibility of business" was to make money legitimately.

Companies, the "Friedman doctrine" reasoned, could only profit *sustainably* by delivering ever-better products and services at ever-better prices. This required treating employees well enough to attract and retain them, and doing no harm: neither deceiving customers, breaking the law, nor injuring third parties (polluting). This made it impossible to serve shareholders without also serving society.

By 2019, this argument was taking water. Offshoring had devastated communities, even regions. Corporate lobbying had made many laws governing companies seem unfair or ineffective, particularly regarding the environment and competition. Voters were skeptical that legitimate profit-seeking necessarily led to positive social outcomes, especially in the wake of the 2008 financial crisis. The Republican Party, long "the party of Big Business," had come to house some of big business' most vocal critics.

Against this backdrop the BRT expanded its members' concerns to include the needs of employees, suppliers, and communities. "While each of our individual companies serves its own corporate purpose," its revision stated, "we share a fundamental commitment to all of our stakeholders."

If signatories expected general acclaim, however, they were soon disappointed.

Scattered applause came from some corners. The *New York Times* marveled at the "break with decades of corporate orthodoxy." The *Wall Street Journal* called the move "a major philosophical shift." Some academics hailed it as "a milestone" in business history, as well as "a sign of the times."

Others saw this new stance less as leadership than catch-up. In light of corporate America's failings, interest in the purpose of companies—and of the individuals who worked for them—had surged to unimaginable heights. Since Google began tracking online queries in 2004, searches for "business purpose" and its new shorthand, "WHY," had grown more than tenfold.

Against this backdrop, the BRT's shift seemed to many "generic" and "rhetorical," little more than "a marketing ploy."

Three years later, JUST Capital, a nonprofit promoting corporate responsibility, took stock of the statement's impact on stakeholder perceptions. The poll's findings were perplexing. Less than half believed companies were actively "promoting an economy that serves all Americans," let alone "building an economy that allows each person to succeed through hard work and creativity." Only a slim majority believed companies were "building an economy that allows each person to lead a life of meaning and dignity." And all three figures were falling.

At the same time, BRT members had achieved meaningful gains

in JUST's social responsibility scores, increasing their share of the "JUST 100" from 49 percent to 62 percent.

What was going on?

WHY COMPANIES CARE ABOUT WHY

"Did you ever expect a corporation to have a conscience, when it has no soul to be damned, and no body to be kicked?"

England's top law officer in the late 1700s, Lord Chancellor Edward Thurlow, has proven to be far from alone in questioning companies' commitment to the common good. It's not hard to see why. Corporations may be "artificial persons," subject to the laws of the land like any real person. Yet the dynamics of how they operate in practice—notably insulating their human representatives from accountability for corporate malfeasance—often stretch the analogy to a breaking point.

So why have we come to see these soulless entities engage in so much soul-searching lately, articulating not only inspiring missions and visions but ethical credos and values statements?

The short answer dates back not to Peter Drucker's 1973 "call to purpose" (see preface) but to an article published almost twenty years earlier. MIT economist Robert Solow's "A Contribution to the Theory of Economic Growth" demonstrated how changes in productivity (output per hour worked) contributed to economies' long-term growth, driving increases in wages, employment, and living standards.

No sooner did productivity growth become a primary focus for macroeconomists and policymakers, however, than something shocking happened.

It began to fall.

⌐━

In retrospect, outsize productivity growth was to be expected after World War II. Peace meant not only recovery from wartime

constraints but also the arrival of new and more efficient technological and process improvements developed during the war, which
also contributed to record productivity growth that tripled by the
mid-1950s.

Few expected that the measure would stagnate over the next two
decades before beginning a steady decline, interrupted only briefly by
the commercialization of the internet around the turn of the century
(Exhibit 1.1). By the early 2010s, productivity growth across advanced
economies languished at around 1 percent, a level not seen in the US
since after the Civil War. A decade later, the figure had fallen below zero
in many countries, the miserable conclusion of a seventy-year slide.

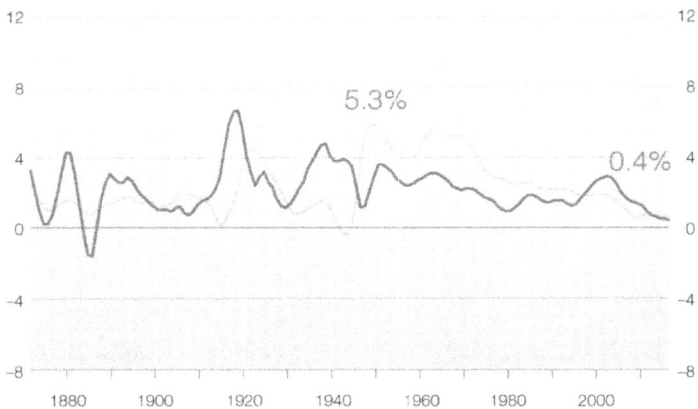

Productivity defined as GDP per hour worked. Calculated using Hodrick-Prescott filter. Drawn from similar
analysis in Martin Neil Baily and Nicholas Montalbano, Why is productivity growth so slow? Possible
explanations and policy responses, Brookings Institution, September 2016. See technical appendix for details
on methodology. Figures may not sum, because of rounding.

Source: A. Bergeaud, G. Cette, and R. Lecat, "Productivity trends in advanced countries between 1890 and
2012," Review of Income and Wealth, volume 62, number 3, 2015; McKinsey Global Institute analysis

Exhibit 1.1: Average advanced country and US productivity growth since 1860.
Source: McKinsey

Solow's theory suggested such decline would be accompanied by
despair. Without productivity increases to pay for it, real wage growth
(wage growth adjusted for inflation) would be expected to stall. Succes-

sive generations would notice they weren't seeing the improvements in living standards their parents and grandparents had enjoyed. Widespread resentment and social unrest would follow.

Reality turned out to be even worse. From the 1970s, as shareholder activism took hold, wage increases fell even faster than productivity (Exhibit 1.2). Combined with rampant offshoring and outsize inflation in sectors associated with lifestyle improvement (housing, health care, and higher education), early twenty-first-century workers became the first peacetime generation in memory to feel poorer as adults than they had as kids.

Hand-wringing lessened during the early months of the pandemic, when the trend appeared to reverse. As companies laid off workers and sought to make do with less, productivity growth spiked. But the reprieve was temporary. In early 2022, the US recorded negative productivity growth (minus 1.7 percent) for the first time since tracking began.

Disconnect between productivity and a typical worker's compensation, 1948–2014

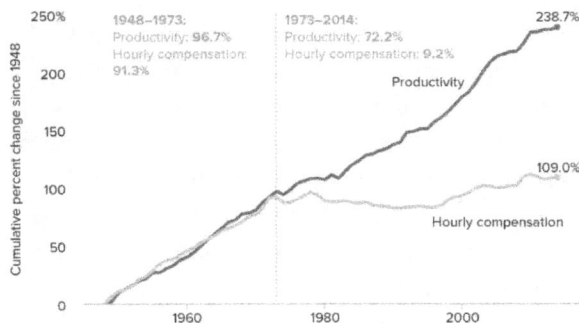

1948–1973:
Productivity: **96.7%**
Hourly compensation:
91.3%

1973–2014:
Productivity: 72.2%
Hourly compensation: 9.2%

238.7%

Productivity

109.0%

Hourly compensation

Cumulative percent change since 1948

Note: Data are for average hourly compensation of production/nonsupervisory workers in the private sector and net productivity of the total economy. "Net productivity" is the growth of output of goods and services minus depreciation per hour worked.

Source: EPI analysis of data from the BEA and BLS (see technical appendix for more detailed information)

Exhibit 1.2: Real wage growth versus productivity growth, 1948–2014
Source: Economic Policy Institute

Later that year, the founder and co-CEO of one of the century's most successful companies, Salesforce's Marc Benioff, took to his company's Slack feed in anguish:

How do we increase the productivity of our employees at Salesforce? New employees (hired during the pandemic in 2021 & 2022) are especially facing much lower productivity. Is this a reflection of our office policy? Are we not building tribal knowledge with new employees without an office culture? Are our managers not directly addressing productivity with their teams? Are we not investing enough time into our new employees? Do managers focus enough time and energy on onboarding new employees & achieving productivity? Is coming as a new employee to Salesforce too overwhelming?

Coming from a productivity software company, such questions conveyed how deeply leaders had come to be preoccupied with a new concern—the notion that employee mindset, often seen as a nice-to-have intangible, could impact something as critical as productivity. Benioff made no reference to information technologies, proprietary or otherwise, nor to any of the other productivity killers that economists typically bemoaned: outsourcing, restructuring, weak demand projection, and poor capacity optimization. Tellingly, he focused on the "soft" drivers of productivity growth that HR professionals had long worried about. Culture. Knowledge sharing. Onboarding. Fit.

He was far from alone. Around the same time, an unusual workplace study began to catch leaders' attention. In 2018, the digital coupon platform Vouchercloud had investigated the productivity question from the bottom up, asking two thousand UK office workers how they spent their time. Reported activities included engaging on social media, shopping online, and making hot drinks—fair enough. What shocked was the average time per day spent on activities they were paid to do: two hours and 53 minutes, just 36 percent of a typical eight-hour shift.

In one respect, this finding confirmed managers' worst fears. In another, however, it gave them hope—for it pointed to a solution.

"Employee engagement," a term coined by a 1990 Boston University study, refers to how connected workers feel to their work, colleagues, and employers. Having been found to correlate with key performance measures like employee turnover and productivity, online interest in the subject has grown more than fivefold since 2004. The curious have included more than disgruntled employees and worried HR managers. Hard-nosed leaders have increasingly come to see what many find to be an uncomfortably "touchy-feely" factor as a key to reviving flagging productivity growth. It's not hard to see how motivating workers to invest just a few more minutes in productive work activity day might create significant value.

Alas, engagement has proven to be almost as mysterious as the ill it promises to cure. Internal studies are often distorted. Employees fear revealing their lack of commitment to bosses, even in anonymous surveys, resulting in rosier-than-actual readings.

Gallup's State of the Global Workplace report, which has become the gold standard of engagement across companies, has been more helpful—and sobering. Its first edition in 2012 found that only 13 percent of employees in 142 countries outside the US felt engaged at work. The US figure was much higher, but still just 30 percent. A decade later, the global figure had climbed, but only to a still-dismaying 23 percent, with the US effectively unchanged.

Leaders generally avoid discussing such findings with staff for fear of making things worse: the disengaged are unlikely to take heart by learning many colleagues have also checked out. Privately, however, many have come to see engagement as the puzzle they urgently need to solve to revive productivity growth—and they believe the answer has something to do with WHY.

WHY EMPLOYEES CARE

September 2009: a fine evening in the picturesque Seattle suburb of Newcastle, Washington. A bespectacled marketing executive from London steps onto a modest stage before a few dozen curious faces to talk about the subject of his first book, coming out the following month. Eighteen minutes later, he steps down to rapturous applause—though few at this TEDx event truly appreciate what they've just witnessed.

In the decade that follows, the talk will garner close to 100 million views, making it the third most popular TED Talk ever. The book, *Start With WHY: How Great Leaders Inspire Everyone to Take Action*, will sell over a million copies, topping bestseller lists and being translated into dozens of languages. By 2023, daily searches for its subject will have increased fourfold. The very language used to discuss it changes: "WHY" in all caps, effectively replaces "business purpose" in common usage (Exhibit 1.3).

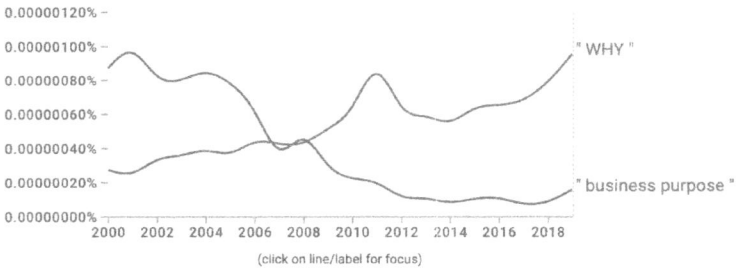

Exhibit 1.3: Uses of "WHY" and "business purpose" in print, 2000–2019
Source: Google Ngram Viewer

Simon Sinek has literally changed the way we talk about purpose. His impact on how we actually live it, however, has turned out to be rather less profound. As we've seen, a decade and a half after he took to that stage, less than one in six frontline managers and employees report feeling their WHY at work. From 2012 to 2023, the needle on employee engagement in the US, where most of those books were sold, moved up only 1 percent—statistically flat. Bosses who have tried to follow his prescriptions, like our friends at WowCo (preface), typically wonder if it has something to do with them—or, less charitably, if it's all B.S.

Before we can understand what hasn't worked, we need to unpack exactly what *Start With Why* has tapped into. Why did employee interest in purpose explode as it did after 2009?

A good place to start is with a more general question: Why do we talk about anything?

It well may be because we're newly enthused by the subject, as with a new job, relationship, or social trend, like "love" in the '60s. Yet often it's because of the opposite, as the counterculture philosopher Alan Watts noted. "When an organ is working properly, you don't feel it," he said. But if you're suddenly going on about, say, your vision? "You've got cataracts." As a society, we can easily get hung up on something that's not working, like "peace" in the '60s.

By the measure of Google's search and print databases, we now spend more time talking about why we go to work than any previous generation. Surveys suggest this is not because we're feeling elated about our jobs. They simply aren't delivering what we've come to expect or hope they should.

An essential question is why—and what we can do about it.

In Part Two, we shall peel the onion to reveal what we really mean by "purpose" or "WHY," why it matters to us as employees, and how this intersects with the WHY of companies. In Part Three, we shall explore how a more in-depth understanding of purpose might enable greater alignment of company and employee needs, and more promising practices for driving it.

Before we can do so, however, it helps to understand exactly how we've come to find ourselves beset by disconnects between our aspirations as individuals and our objectives as leaders, and where solutions to connect the two have failed.

In short, we could use a bit of history. ᴏ┓

KEY TAKEAWAYS   ⌐╍

1. Twenty-first century managers and employees care about WHY more than any previous generation. Since 2004, online searches for "WHY" and "business purpose" have soared fourfold.

2. Companies care primarily because productivity growth—annual increases in output per hour worked—has been in free fall for 70 years.

3. By one estimate, the average employee is only fully productive for just under three hours a day.

4. Twenty-first century employees have felt the pain of this productivity slump, at a time when real wage growth and living standards are also stagnating.

5. Incoming generations, millennials and Gen Zers, have embraced purpose as another form of reward, but they aren't entirely sure what they're looking for.

6. Simon Sinek's books and talks have changed the language we use to talk about the problem and elevated the need for WHY to the top of employee workplace requirements as well as the management agenda.

7. Sinek's solutions, however, have had limited impact. While employee engagement has risen, it remains around one in five globally and under one in three in the US. Moreover, one in six frontline managers and employees say they don't live their purpose at work.

8. We need to understand the disconnects between employee aspirations and leaders' objectives, and the solutions that have failed to bridge the two, by delving into how we got here.

CHAPTER 2

Why Now? How We Got Here

"What we learn from history is that people don't learn from history."

WARREN BUFFETT

T HE SPEAKER HAD JUST FINISHED ADDRESSING the leadership forum when an attendee approached.

His talk, "Making Missions Matter," had provoked lively discussion. Half the companies represented—enterprises with revenues over $100 million—hadn't previously seen value in purpose statements. Most that had tried had seen little return on their investment.

After hearing about an alternative approach, several were now comparing notes.

"Sylvia" had a different question. As incoming CEO of a young biotech firm, she felt it was too soon to refresh the vision and mission she'd inherited. But this wasn't what she wanted to talk about.

Sylvia wanted to talk about her dad.

"Bob" had recently retired after forty-three years with a community bank, having started as a teller and worked his way up to regional manager. As a summer intern in her teens, Sylvia had been shocked to discover her father's days were all pretty much the same. He arrived at 9:30 a.m., dealt with issues from the previous day, talked to customers and staff, and rolled out eight hours later.

Two hundred and fifty days a year over forty-odd years—ten thousand nearly identical days—that had been Bob's career.

The speaker wasn't sure he heard a question.

"The thing is," Sylvia said, "he was always happy. He loved his job."

And?

"Well, he never once felt he had to talk about his WHY."

Ah.

Like other leaders, Sylvia had no trouble with the idea that inspired employees might be more engaged and productive. On the contrary, she found the idea so persuasive that only one thought gave her pause:

Why have we only started to talk about this *now?*

The short answer is that we haven't. The articulation-centric way we currently approach business purpose may be only decades old. The idea that corporations have a critical place in society, however, is older than the legal institution itself. And the notion that individuals have specific roles to play at work? Evolutionary biologists say that's prehistoric.

In Part Two we'll turn out attention to what psychologists and economists have come to see as the key aspects of employee and company activity that relate to purpose. To fully appreciate and build upon their insights, however, we must consider how our understanding and feeling of WHY has come to be problematic at all.

HOW EMPLOYEES GOT HERE

Across centuries and cultures and disciplines, from Aristotle to zoologists, students of nature have largely agreed: living beings' highest goal is a state of well-being we might call happiness. For humans, achieving this is complicated by a distinctive capability we can't turn off: our ability to remember or imagine states different from our present, and thus form expectations.

The University College London's Happiness Project has found expectations to be one of the greatest factors in determining our sense of well-being. Too high or low, and we feel miserable. Leading to a critical question: How do we form expectations?

The field of language philosophy that emerged in the 1920s provides a compelling answer. It holds that words are not simply a representation of something we are already thinking or feeling, but tools that actually shape our perceptions.

Consider this: Before we learn the words "good" and "kid," then put them together, few of us are particularly concerned about being one.* After that, however, we spend much of our lives trying to be a better if not the best version of whatever labels we've taken on, from parent to friend to our current job title.

Along the way, most of us wonder if we're doing it right. Questions creep in:

Who am I?

Why am I here?

What should I be doing with my life?

For most of our history as self-aware Homo sapiens, the answers to these questions were relatively easy to come by for one simple reason: We didn't have much choice. With limited social mobility or life options, there was little point in thinking about what our WHY might be. Our purpose was set in the middle French-derived sense of the term: what we were "put forward" to do by our social hierarchies. The most we might be able to achieve was within our born rank—to be the best lord or vassal we could be, unless we had the opportunity to step out of the system by joining a religious order.

No point, then, in giving the matter much thought.

This general fatalism began to ebb with the Industrial Revolution. New technologies created new industries that reshaped the job market.

---

* This is exemplified in the story disability rights advocate Helen Keller told of the day she acquired language, portrayed in the film *The Miracle Worker* (1962), when she did not regret tearing an object to pieces until she learned it was a "doll."

Increasing wealth expanded career options. It became possible to leave the family or local economy for something better paying elsewhere.

The twentieth-century brought further choice. Wars drew men into military roles, opening paths for women in the civilian workforce. The need for immigrant labor began breaking down geographic and racial barriers. Rising incomes among marginalized groups created new educational and career opportunities. Class barriers weakened. We edged toward a world where it seemed to some, like the 1940s memoirist Betty MacDonald, that "anybody can do anything."

All this turned out to have an unexpected flip side: When it came to choice, more was not necessarily better. Within a decade of MacDonald's exuberant cry, researchers like Bell Labs's William Baker and the economist Herbert Simon noticed that consumers now faced a challenge their less affluent forebears hadn't: the risk of making big purchasing decisions they regretted. The novel anxiety that ensued spread into other areas of life, from where to live and whom to marry to what education to pursue and what job to take. At the end of the century, psychologist Barry Schwartz saw this "paradox of choice" as the defining bugbear of modern life.

How have we dealt with this challenge? By seeking advice. From 2000 to 2021, the number of life coaches and financial planners in the US more than doubled. Spending on therapists and other aids to mental wellness tripled. In 2022, Americans bought almost twice as many self-help books each month than they did in the *whole* of 1990.

Is it any accident that our fascination with WHY blossomed at the same time?

PURPOSE GAPS

"People don't buy what you do. They buy WHY you do it."

Simon Sinek's 2009 sound bite has proven not only powerful—revolutionary-sounding yet seemingly intuitive—but evidence of its author's marketing roots.

Some have pushed back. Is our primary concern as human beings *really* to sell ourselves to others, or simply to feel better? Does, say, Elon Musk's passion for social media make X more attractive than Twitter? If so, why are user numbers falling?

Whatever your view, there's little doubt broad acceptance of Sinek's claim has shaped much of the modern purpose conversation. Since 2018, brand expert Afdhel Aziz has maintained a popular survey of surveys that he calls "the business case for purpose," which demonstrates just how central a marketing mindset has become to our thinking about WHY. Much of it details research on how consumer perceptions of a brand's WHY impact everything from price premiums and interest in new products to customer advocacy and loyalty. When considering employees, the focus is less on work itself than how social impact considerations inform decisions to join (i.e., buy into) a company. One study finds that 63 percent of millennials would only join one with "a strong CSR (Corporate Social Responsibility) policy," while another calls Gen Z "the first generation to prioritize purpose over salary."

The compendium reveals far less about the impact of purpose *after* employees come to work, on things like engagement, productivity, and well-being. Indeed, the whole question of just how much companies are investing in WHY—refreshing mission statements, for example—emerges as something of a research blind spot.

Such proxies as can be found seem tenuous. From 1990 to 2019, spending on "cause marketing" related to a company's core operations grew almost three times faster than general corporate citizenship, which may imply more internal engagement—or it may not. Perhaps more telling is that the popularity of the search term "WHY workshop" has risen more than sevenfold since 2009.

Is such spending moving the needle on employee engagement?

Perhaps the most penetrating insight here comes from a pair of workplace studies conducted months apart in 2020, which used the same term to describe distinct, and dismaying, discoveries.

In a survey of 1,500 employees and 500 business leaders, PwC found that while 54 percent of firms defined "a clear and relevant purpose," only 13 percent explained how purpose was embedded in their business models. It called this difference between talk and walk "the Purpose Gap", and warned of its dangers: Such discrepancies led six in ten employees to disengage.

McKinsey used the same term to describe its own finding in a survey of 1,021 individuals. While 85 percent of "upper managers" said they could "live their purpose at work," only 15 percent of "front-line managers and employees" agreed. Since upper management represented less than 2 percent of the workforce, this suggested that less than one in six of all working people felt purpose at work.

McKinsey cautioned leaders to mind *this* Purpose Gap, framing the takeaway in terms of the War for Talent the firm identified two decades earlier. Sixty-three percent of respondents wanted "more opportunities for purpose in their day-to-day work." Companies needed to help them find it—"or watch them leave."

Living your purpose in day-to-day work, % of respondents

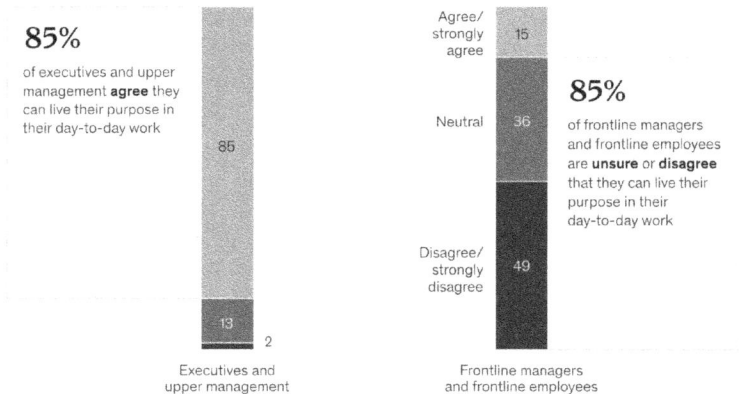

85%
of executives and upper management **agree** they can live their purpose in their day-to-day work

85

13

2

Executives and
upper management

Agree/
strongly
agree   15

Neutral   36

85%
of frontline managers
and frontline employees
are **unsure** or **disagree**
that they can live their
purpose in their
day-to-day work

Disagree/
strongly
disagree   49

Frontline managers
and frontline employees

Source: McKinsey Individual Purpose survey, August 2020 (n = 1,021)

Exhibit 2.1: The purpose gap
Source: McKinsey

If this was not sufficiently alarming, pandemic data soon followed to suggest companies were facing a Great Resignation. Record numbers were quitting not only their jobs, but the market. The US labor participation rate (those working or seeking work as a percentage of the working-age population) fell to levels not seen since the 1970s, when statisticians began counting women as workers.

Among those who stayed at their desks, a new phenomenon—arguably more significant—came to light. The productivity spike triggered by pandemic belt-tightening not only faded, but went negative. So another new term entered the lexicon: Quiet Quitting.

Retaining talent was now only one of management's concerns. In a historically tight labor market, the question that shot to the top of the agenda was how to inspire discretionary effort: a question that went not only to the heart of the productivity puzzle, but the essence of human well-being.

HOW COMPANIES GOT HERE

In August 2022, three journalists on *The Ezra Klein Show* podcast tackled another workplace trend: the rise of remote work.

When one lamented the loss of social interaction in the office, another suggested the very need was tragic:

> *It should not be our employer who is solving our loneliness problems… It's a sad state of affairs when we are relying uniquely on our employers as our social hub in any capacity.*

None seemed aware of this claim's unintended irony. As their very name implies, companies have always been social hubs. At first blush, the most common definitions of "company" might seem at odds:

1. A commercial business, e.g., "a shipping company"
4. The fact or condition of being with another or others, especially in a way that provides friendship and enjoyment, e.g., "I could do with some company."

Originally, however, these referred to almost the same thing. The word's Latin roots, *com* and *panis*, mean "with" and "bread", respectively. "Company" crept into use in the twelfth century to refer to groups of individuals who ate and worked together.

The definition began to split when initially informal working groups began to enjoy legal protection: the ability to raise money collectively, have their assets protected by the state, and limit members' personal liability when things went wrong.

States wanted to know what they were protecting. Accordingly, the earliest "corporations" in medieval Europe were what we might now call "special-purpose vehicles," with their aims spelled out in founding charters.*As early modern entrepreneurs began raising their sights, however, corporate purposes started to blur. In the 1600s, corporations became states' preferred vehicle for backing overseas expeditions. The earliest ventures had names indicating the regions they aimed to exploit: The Dutch East India Company, The Hudson's Bay Company, The Virginia Company, and so on.

These enterprises quickly outgrew the pots in which they'd been planted. Shareholders wanted greater returns, and the price was focus. By the end of its first century, Dutch East India had operations stretching from Indonesia to Africa, diversified from trading into adjunct sectors like farming, shipping, and venture capital.

Back home, manufacturing and merchant guilds began demanding the same protections as their seafaring counterparts, and proved to be every bit as opportunistic. Northern Europe's Hanseatic League evolved from a trade association into a leading international bank, even a military power in its own right.

In the wake of the Industrial Revolution arose capital markets that further changed the game. Growing wealth produced a broader sector of profit-hungry yet inattentive shareholders. Companies successful in one sector could easily raise the money to enter others.

Within a century they were no longer confined to the low-hang-

---

* The earliest were large public works projects that required substantial financing and might be expected to take generations to complete, like cathedrals and roads. Some argue that the "shreni" or guilds formed in India in the fourth century BCE had similar protections, much like European corporations; but that is a parallel history, lacking a direct line of descent to the modern company.

ing fruit of adjacent sectors. Ready capital put unprecedented temptation into leaders' hands, given the ability to go into any business, anywhere. The resulting "conglomerates"—named after an engineering term for incongruous materials rolled into a ball—eschewed focus as a matter of principle. The electrical product company Thomas Edison founded in 1889 showed far more interest in being "General" than "Electric," spending its first century moving into fields as unrelated as transportation, health care, finance, and television.

The conglomerate boom continued after World War II, creating yet more "multinationals" that barely understood the markets where they played. But the trend soon ran its course. Local pushback became a political headache. Operational complexity made planning difficult. Most significantly, valuations suffered. Assessing companies with fingers in so many pies was challenging; it was hard to tell which were generating or eating cash. Diversification began to look like investors' job, not managers'.

Not coincidentally, the period from the mid-1960s to the early 1980s saw an obscure economic term become a business buzzword. "Value creation" referred to generating returns for shareholders in the form of dividends and share price growth. As markets entered prolonged bear territory—from 1966 to 1982, the S&P fell almost 75 percent—pressure grew on companies to create value not by reallocating capital among businesses but by operating individual businesses well.

It was against this backdrop that Peter Drucker issued his 1973 challenge to managers to explain, "What is our business?" His guidance appropriated a term until then used almost exclusively by evangelists, the military, and, oddly, news organizations:

A business is not defined by its name, statutes, or articles of incorporation. It is defined by the business mission. Only a clear definition of the mission and purpose of the organization makes possible clear and realistic business objectives.

This thought took root among the most forward-thinking and

best-resourced organizations. From Fortune 500 boardrooms to the *Harvard Business Review*, practitioners and students of management celebrated the power and promise of mission statements, debating the best ways to craft them. By 2000, "mission statement" was being used over thirty times more often in print than in 1972.

HOW MANAGEMENT GOT HERE

Social media has taught us a lot about what makes something "go viral." Viral content provokes a two-pronged emotional response: to arouse (or surprise), and to convey a positive (reassuring or inspiring) message. This rests on cultural context, common beliefs, and preoccupations.

The virality of mission statements toward the end of the twentieth century, and of "WHY" a decade later, thus raises a critical question: What paved the way for such an enthusiastic reception?

It's necessary but insufficient to grasp the history of companies as social institutions, as we have just done. We need to better understand the evolving mindset and those tasked with running companies.

Management is the process of coordinating the function and behavior of individuals to achieve objectives.

Its norms and practices down the centuries have hinged largely on practitioners' working model of human psychology: that is, how bosses think their charges can be motivated.

Inspired in part by the work of Columbia Business School's Rita Gunther McGrath, we can distill the history of management into three eras, each defined by a different understanding of worker motvation. Through this we can begin to see how WHY has come to play such a prominent role in the twenty-first century workplace.

Model 1: Physical

The origins of the word "management" itself are less respectable than modern management schools might want us to think.

The term was coined in the world of medieval horse training. *Manus* is Latin for "hand." An animal that could be "managed" was one that could be controlled "by the hand," typically one holding a whip.

"Management" drifted into the world of human work because bosses saw workers as similar to those long-suffering equines: mindless, lazy, capable of little more than simple routines, responsive only to threats of physical pain.* The practice, thus, looked more like something we might see on *The Sopranos* than *The Office*. Poor performance was less likely to be addressed with feedback than beatings.

Eighteenth-century managers were so focused on leveraging new technologies quickly that few stopped to question whether such techniques were moral, efficient, or even effective.

Slavery became colonial overseers' preferred form of labor. Factory heads became responsible not just for workers they could physically oversee, but for hundreds toiling out of sight, too.

This begged a new question: What could inspire effort when the boss was away? The answer fell in line with previous practice: fear of physical punishment if caught slacking. Sticks were familiar, easy, and cheaper than carrots.

In the late nineteenth century, the American engineer Frederick Taylor brought stopwatches into the mix, calling this "scientific management." But the basic mindset was unchanged. The notion that workers might be able to think and want to work was inconvenient, troubling, and thus unimaginable.

Model 2: Mental

The labor and violent upheavals of the early twentieth century threw such assumptions into question.

---

* Of course, they did not see *themselves* this way, relying instead on class and racial prejudices to justify their abuse.

The seeds of a new model were planted far from the factory floor, at a liberal arts college in Brooklyn. At the height of World War II, psychologist Abraham Maslow sought to develop a view of human nature that treated us not as perennially broken "bags of symptoms" but as beings capable of growth, progress and happiness. This, he hoped, would help put the brakes on the sense of mass dissatisfaction that inspired war. Maslow identified and ranked the ingredients of mental and emotional well-being. Once we felt assured of basic physical needs like security and sustenance, he believed, we would hunger for "higher order" needs like inner peace.

One of the most fertile grounds for Maslow's soon-to-be-famous hierarchy of needs turned out to be a business school. MIT's Douglas McGregor spent much of the 1950s mapping the hierarchy's management implications into what would turn out to be one of the century's most influential business books.

The Human Side of Enterprise distinguished two models of worker motivation. The traditional "Theory X" took employees to be fundamentally lazy, motivated only by extrinsic rewards and punishments. The rising "Theory Y," however, saw them as thinking beings capable of enjoying work intrinsically and taking pride in their output.

McGregor's speculation dovetailed with another emerging theory that traced the rise of "knowledge work" not to psychological but technological progress. Peter Drucker believed an increasing share of modern economies relied on mental rather than physical skill and motivation. Employees' value thus came from processing information, rather than simply performing rote tasks.

The line Drucker attempted to draw around "knowledge" professions like law and finance, however, quickly blurred. Readers could not help wondering if functions like sales, which involved, among other things, acting as the eyes and ears of an organization, deciding which data was worth gathering and relaying, might not also be considered "information processing." Indeed, what about line workers, assistants, even receptionists, who might spot problems and propose solutions? Without meaning to do so, Drucker had inspired yet another perspective, one that saw virtually *all* functions of an organization as intrinsically rewarding, Theory Y-aligned, knowledge work.

In the following decades, some business leaders consciously tacked toward Theory Y. Pressed to explain the Japanese Miracle— the astonishing transformation of a war-wrecked, semi-industrial power into the world's second-largest economy—Panasonic founder Kōnosuke Matsushita explained that superior business performance required turning the principles of scientific management on their head.

"Your firms are built on the [Frederick] Taylor model," he told an American researcher:

Even worse, so are your heads. With your bosses doing the thinking while workers wield the screwdrivers, you're convinced deep down that it is the right way to run a business. [Yet] the essence of management is getting out of the heads of the bosses, and into the heads of labor.

Model 3: Emotional

Few anticipated the next progression in managers' model of motivation—that there might be as much value in employees' hearts as their heads.

The information and digital revolutions of the late twentieth century enabled new heights of corporate innovation. They also bestowed new potential upon anyone who now came to work to find a PC on their desk.

Competitive advantage shifted from simply producing better information to acting on it: turning data into insights that would lead to better products and services, faster.

This lined up neatly with Drucker's call to purpose. He'd matched that proposal with the view that the objective companies shared was "to create and keep a customer." This meant "the business enterprise has two, and only two, basic functions: marketing and innovation."

A quarter century later, leaders had come to see marketing and innovation as two sides of the same process: what the "grandfather of Silicon Valley venture capital," Sequoia Capital founder Don Valentine, called "product-market fit." But these were not created equal.

For marketer Seth Godin, differentials in practical control over each element implied it was foolhardy to focus on finding customers for one's products. Rather, companies should "find products for their customers."

Exhibit 2.2: Feeling cool: The first iPhone customer
Source: Reuters

Fast-growing '90s brands like Apple and Starbucks piled on further insight. When customers purchase products or services, Starbucks' CEO Howard Schultz observed, they were really purchasing an experience or emotional state, like pride, comfort, confidence, or simply feeling cool.

Godin pushed this further. The role of a company was not to deliver just *any* experience, he suggested, but to help customers achieve goals they might not fully understand themselves. "Marketing is our quest to make change on behalf of those we serve," he wrote.

"We do it by understanding the irrational forces that drive each of us."

All told, the "knowledge" in knowledge work began to seem less like the product of logic and experience than of what researchers Peter Salavoy and John Mayer had named "emotional intelligence" (EI) in 1990: the ability to leverage one's own emotions into empathy, insight, and communication.

EI was even harder to direct in the top-down style Matsushita had critiqued. If Godin and Schultz were right—if businesses had to connect with customers on the level of latent emotional needs—managers had to operationalize an unfamiliar blend of so-called soft skills: empathy, anticipation, collaboration, and communication.

This had to be an all-hands-on-deck endeavor. Sales and service might be a company's eyes and ears. But the data and hypotheses they relayed meant little without the perspectives of product development, operations, and finance determining what was economically, operationally, or even technologically feasible.

In this context, interest in Drucker's "business purpose" and "missions"—stripped of reference to or even memory of the author himself—skyrocketed.

No matter how astute, these observations remained mere sparks. What fanned them into flames, driving a transformation in management culture, was a watershed technological transformation that arrived at just the right moment.

The late 1980s invention of a computer information management system called the World Wide Web radically broadened the usability and accessibility of a computer network dating back to the 1960s known as the internet, transforming the latter into a new frontier for commerce.

For many, the dot-com boom did more than create a new sales channel. It turned the laws of business on their head. Companies had to innovate at increasing speeds or be left in the dust of a scrappy start-up. E-commerce entrepreneurs took corporate visions to be not just helpful tools but indispensable assets. From venture capital to public markets, businesses new and old became measured by the same yardstick—not just their innovative products nor burgeoning customer bases, but the plans they had to grow and change the world.

Purpose was ready for its close-up.

HOW WE GOT WHYS

At the dawn of the twenty-first century, leaders saw value creation in a new light, resting on two fresh and related ideas: the benefits of a visionary connection with shareholders, and the necessity of emotional connection with customers.

This brings us close to answering the question Sylvia raised about her dad at the start of this chapter. The prospect of generating outsize personal wealth by changing the world gave individuals far more interest in purpose than previous generations.

Now, they just had to figure out how the thing worked.

Good to Great

First to the plate was Stanford professor Jim Collins. From the mid-1990s, Collins led a five-year study into the practices that turned "good" companies (those that outperformed the market over many years) into "great" ones (those that managed to do even better for even longer). The resulting work, *Good to Great: Why Some Companies Make the Leap…and Others Don't,* turned out to be one of the most widely read management handbooks of all time. Since its 2001 publication, it has sold more than three million copies, winning praise from the *Wall Street Journal*'s CEO Council as "one of the best business books ever written."

A central factor of "greatness," Collins and his team discovered, was a company's ability to focus on "doing one thing well." Inspired by an Aesop fable about a hedgehog and a fox beset by gadflies—the former able to protect itself by simply rolling into a ball, the latter using several partial measures that failed—Collins dubbed this "the Hedgehog Concept." A company could find its "Hedgehog" at the intersection of three factors: how it made money, the passions its people shared, and a vision of what it "could be the best in the world at."

Three Circles of the Hedgehog Concept

Exhibit 2.3: The Hedgehog Concept
Source: Jim Collins

Such focus did not simply make companies great. It also elevated the individuals who worked for them. When these factors aligned, Collins claimed:

> [N]ot only does your work move toward greatness, but so does your life. For, in the end, it is impossible to have a great life unless it is a meaningful life. And it is very difficult to have a meaningful life without meaningful work.

Hedgehog exercises gradually became a standard tool among companies looking to renew their strategies, including articulating their missions and visions. This raised new questions. Was business purpose a cause of greatness? An effect? Or both?

Drive

Like Collins, vice-presidential speechwriter turned author Daniel Pink didn't set out to write about purpose. His 2009 *Drive: The Surprising Truth About What Motivates Us* explored the drivers and implications of a striking finding: sometimes, greater compensation actually *weakened* performance. Pink wanted to know what really motivated work.

Behavioral psychology research, much of it inspired by Maslow, suggested that our psychological "operating system" had changed over the course of human history. In prehistoric cultures, we were motivated primarily by the desire to survive: what Pink called Motivation 1.0. Civilization enabled us to accumulate wealth and status: Motivation 2.0.

Yet these drivers remained extrinsic to work itself. Employees could find themselves rewarded for work they found mind-numbing, degrading, even harmful. What had changed the game again were the technological transformations of the late twentieth century. More or less assured of material security, Pink argued workers in developed economies had shifted their focus to other considerations:

- "Autonomy," the dignity of acting under their own direction as much as possible;
- "Mastery," the feeling of excelling at what they do; and
- "Purpose," "the service of some greater objective."

Pink provided little further definition or guidance on the last point. Still, *Drive* sold over a million copies, became standard on managers' bookshelves, and promoted "Purpose" to the top of the HR agenda, alongside Drucker's missions and Collins's hedgehogs.

Meanwhile, a lesser-known author was about to lift its profile even higher.

The Golden Circle

Start With WHY's overnight success around the same time owed much to Simon Sinek's experience as a marketing executive. Its basic framework had all the hallmarks of a viral idea: surprising, reassuring, and easy to share.

The book presented a simplified representation of a human brain (since found to be highly persuasive to readers) to argue that human beings were motivated more by emotion than calculation. Our inner limbic brain was said to be the seat of emotion, the core of our thinking. Analytical reasoning and articulation lived in our outer, seemingly less primal, neocortex.

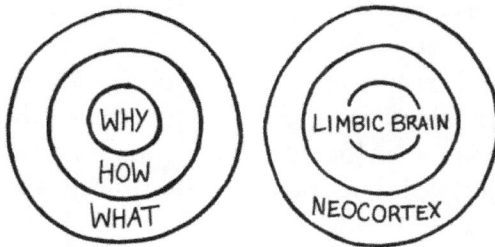

Exhibit 2.4: The Golden Circle and the brain
Source: Simon Sinek

This did not need to be accurate, psychologically or evolutionarily, to resonate. For many, it made intuitive sense that we should be governed more by emotion than reason, and that the way we think about our jobs and companies should align with the nested circles Sinek called The Golden Circle.

The subtitle, *How Great Leaders Inspire Everyone to Take Action*, spoke volumes. Sinek was not selling strategy or productivity. His objective was simply to motivate. Like any good marketer, his focus was on how to sell a product—and the most important product was you.

Proof

Among *Good to Great*'s most resonant findings was its notion that great leaders engaged in "reality-based thinking," focusing on facts and feasibility rather than wishfulness. (As NFL coach Vince Lombardi is reputed to have said, "Hope is not a strategy.") In this light, many managers remained intuitively uncomfortable steering their businesses on the basis of inspiring words alone. They wanted to be shown the money.

Ex-Procter & Gamble marketing chief Jim Stengel, and a team of analysts from brand consultancy Millward Brown, attempted to do just that. They identified fifty "purpose-driven" companies and contrasted their growth with that of the S&P 500 over a ten-year period.

The results, published in Stengel's 2011 *Grow: How Ideals Power Growth and Profit at the World's Greatest Companies*, were arresting.

While the market had declined slightly, the purpose-driven companies had actually grown by almost 400 percent.

High-profile executives like Facebook COO Sheryl Sandberg applauded Stengel's efforts. Critics, however, alleged cherry-picking. Which companies were "purpose-driven" and which were not were not just subjective but retroactively determined—both research no-nos.

The Stengel 50 Outperforming Brands vs. S&P 500

Stengel Top 50   S&P 500

382.3%

-7.9%

Exhibit 2.5: The Stengel 50 vs. the S&P 500
Source: Jim Stengel, Millward Brown

Contemporary academic studies with more rigorous methodologies looked at objective qualities such as the publication of missions and visions, finding they had limited bottom-line impact.

In the years that followed, new reasons to question not only the impact of purpose but also what the word meant surfaced. Was purpose really the road toward a brighter, more lucrative future? Or was purpose a distraction?

More work was required.

Enter a New Generation

Born between 1980 and the mid 1990s, the first millennials entered the workforce in the early 2000s.

Within a decade, expectations that they might simply behave at work like Gen Xers redux, seeking more independence and growth opportunities, were dashed. A 2016 study identified ways in which millennials' professional motivations and aspirations differed from those who had come before, and now managed them (Exhibit 2.6).

	Past	Future
1	My Paycheck	My Purpose
2	My Satisfaction	My Development
3	My Boss	My Coach
4	My Annual Review	My Ongoing Conversations
5	My Weaknesses	My Strengths
6	My Job	My Life

Exhibit 2.6: Millennials' workplace needs
Source: Gallup, How Millennials Want to Work and Live (2016)

Observers argued several of these were, in fact, different aspects of a single change. Millennials valued purpose so highly—and, thus, sought managerial coaching, development, and ongoing conversations—because, as the report put it, they'd come to see work as "not just a job," but "their life as well."

The drivers of this shift, which Gen Zers appear to share, have been the subject of much commentary. They include younger workers' widespread feeling that—in the face of limited higher education opportunities, lack of affordable housing, and frothy valuations—"all the money has been made," "all the great businesses have happened," and "we'll never live as well as our (boomer) grandparents." Combine these perspectives with a growing cultural focus on social and environmental justice, and it seems only rational to focus less on earning potential than social impact.

Fair enough. But something else seems to be going on as well. Take the Ezra Klein discussion from earlier in this chapter. There's a reason why the concept of workplace as primary social arena may sound more intuitive to younger ears: The rise of social media and mobile phones has changed the way younger workers interact and form friendships, including at school and in our communities. Such trends have made millennials, according to a 2019 YouGov poll, "the loneliest generation," with three in ten reporting "often" or "always" feeling lonely—far more than boomers or Gen Xers. The *Atlantic*'s Derek Thompson calls the resulting attitude "workism," a distinctively (but not uniquely) American life philosophy whose adherents seek their primary social and life meaning in professional activities with almost religious fervor.

Accordingly, when millennials or Gen Zers speak about WHY, purpose, and meaning, it may not be surprising that they're talking about something different than their superiors. Many boomer/Gen X bosses have clung to the orthodoxy that their only real purpose is to serve shareholders: the Friedman doctrine. Younger workers, however, have arrived with different priorities and expectations, including concerns about social justice, corporate citizenship, and environmental impact—and they expected their employers to respect these concerns.

Usage and satisfaction among survey respondents

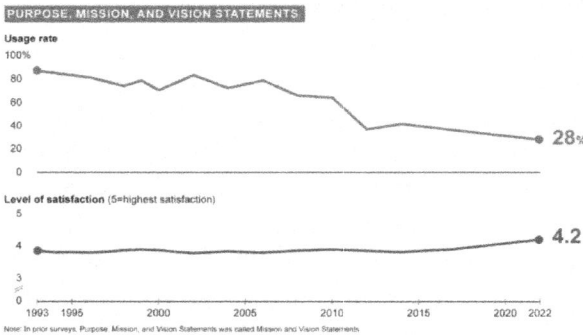

PURPOSE, MISSION, AND VISION STATEMENTS

Usage rate

28%

Level of satisfaction (5=highest satisfaction)

4.2

1993 1995   2000   2005   2010   2015   2020 2022

Note: In prior surveys, Purpose, Mission, and Vision Statements was called Mission and Vision Statements

Exhibit 2.7: Executive usage of and satisfaction with purpose statements
Source: Bain

A striking indicator of this growing malaise has come from Bain & Company. Since 1993, the management consultancy has conducted an annual survey of how leaders felt about and used their mission and vision statements. While respondents have remained consistently satisfied (an average four out of five) with them, usage is a different story. Until 2007, the latter effectively tracked satisfaction, ranging between 70 percent and 90 percent. Since the financial crisis, however, it has plummeted by more than half: In 2022, less than one in three actually used the purpose tools they claim to like more than ever.

Less than half a century after Drucker's rallying cry, interest in business purpose has soared to unimaginable heights, only to hit a ceiling. One Toronto-based HR consultant we work with sees this as

> *a natural growing pain. The very acceptance of purpose as a standard practice has given rise to something previous generations have not had to contend with: expectations.*

The door has been opened. WHY has been let in and legitimized. Now, the question is, how to do it *properly.* ∘⊶

KEY TAKEAWAYS   ⊶

1. The first question we must ask in unraveling our WHY problem is: Why does it seem like we've only just started to care?

2. To answer this question, we must understand how our workplaces became the way they are, and why managers have come to manage them the way they do.

3. Companies began as informal worker associations, at the center of social life—its root words mean "those with whom we break bread."

4. States began to recognize companies as formal "corporations" with charter-specified purposes in order to facilitate financing and allow them to focus on building assets rather than protecting them.

5. Shareholders hungry for returns pressed managers to go beyond their charters; by the late nineteenth century, the most successful companies had become conglomerates operating in many sectors.

6. Challenges in valuing and understanding such complex and wide-spread operations in the late twentieth century led to shareholder pressure for conglomerates to shed unrelated businesses and focus on core, clearly related operations.

7. Against this backdrop, management guru Peter Drucker issued a new rallying cry in 1973: Managers should articulate and follow their "business purpose" or "business mission."

8. Management thinking evolved over the course of three distinct phases, each based on a different understanding of human labor and motivation: physical (human strength, motivated by brute force), mental (knowledge creation, motivated by career contract), and emotional (empathy/emotional intelligence, motivated by purpose). This paved the way for Drucker's call to action to be widely taken up.

9. The twenty-first century pushed the last phase of human labor and motivation forward with three landmark books: Jim Collins's *Good to Great* (2001), which highlighted a focus on purpose as the center of company performance; Daniel Pink's *Drive* (2009),

which included purpose as a core factor of employee motivation; and Simon Sinek's *Start With Why* (2009), which moved purpose front and center.

10. The arrival of millennials in the workplace, who saw little prospect for economic return compared with previous generations, put unprecedented value on the meaning of their work and largely wrote off their managers efforts to be "purpose-driven" as "lip service."

11. While leaders appear broadly satisfied with the purpose statements they've created, less than a third report using them in practice.

PART TWO: *UNDERSTANDING WHY*

"We reason deeply, when we forcibly feel."

MARY WOLLSTONECRAFT
*LETTERS WRITTEN DURING A SHORT RESIDENCE IN
SWEDEN, NORWAY, AND DENMARK* (1796)

CHAPTER 3

What Individuals Want

"The worker does not fulfill himself in his work but denies himself, has a feeling of misery rather than well-being, does not develop freely his mental and physical energies but is physically exhausted and mentally debased. The worker, therefore, feels himself at home only during his leisure time, whereas at work he feels homeless."

KARL MARX

WHAT DOES "DOING PURPOSE PROPERLY" MEAN? The answer depends on what we need it to do.

The fact that most feel they need a WHY suggests it has something to do with our need to feel happy. Before we can map the relationship between purpose and well-being, however, we must remove a stumbling block that advisors and advice seekers alike often trip over:

What are we actually talking about?

In a 2019 interview with author Safi Bahcall, podcaster and author Tim Ferriss despaired over how rarely experts on "soft" managerial practices define their terms. "The discussion can get very nebulous, very quickly," he complained. A topic like culture is "often talked about for two hundred pages in a book without ever defining it."

The same can be said of most purpose experts. Even the person who popularized the term WHY, Simon Sinek, present only a circular definition, equating it with "your cause or belief… [why] you get out of bed in the morning." Daniel Pink calls purpose simply, "something bigger than yourself." Jim Stengel defines it as "the higher order benefit [a business] brings to the world."

Okay. But what kind of bigger something? What's a "higher order benefit"?

For those satisfied with their own definitions, such precision may seem unnecessary. But lack of clarity is a hindrance to a constructive, practical conversation, especially for one that revolves around the intersection of individual and collective WHYs.

Without precision, we may quickly find ourselves working at cross purposes—as it appears we have been.

TOWARD A DEFINITION

"Purpose," life coach Mastin Kipp declared in his 2017 purpose manual *Claim Your Power*:

> *is one of the most overused words in the world of religion, self-help, and personal growth. It's been used so often that it's almost lost its meaning.*

Hear, hear. The world's most popular dictionary, Dictionary. com, lists no fewer than nine definitions, from "the reason for which something exists or is done, made, used, etc." and "an intended or desired result; end; aim; goal" to "practical result, effect, or advantage."

If that isn't enough, its sibling Thesaurus.com suggests dozens of nuances, listing over forty synonyms, from "ambition" and "faith" to "function" and "will." Some are discrete ("meaning," "resolve"). Some overlap ("plan," "wish"). Some are simply opposites ("intention," "outcome").

Is it any surprise so many get muddled?

Aristotle believed that words were our ultimate reality: No knife could ever be as perfectly knife-ish as the word itself. Twentieth-century language philosophers like Ludwig Wittgenstein turned that model on its head. In their view, words don't just describe our tools—they are tools. We use them to get things done. They have no meaning beyond our intentions.

When we're working with any kind of tool, we need to be clear about three things:

a) What we're trying to do with it;
b) What it was designed to do; and
c) What other tool might work better.

For example, we might be making little progress trying to (a) drive screws with a knife that was (b) designed to cut food. It would be better to use (c) a screwdriver, while learning for next time how we slipped into (a) in the first place.

With that in mind, let's look at this word-tool called WHY.

WHAT WE'RE TRYING TO DO WITH WHY

Spend enough hours listening to people talk about their WHY, as we have, and you'll likely experience something like the following.

Ask them why they even care about the topic. After the usual jokes ("Because my manager says I should!"), you'll hear some variation on the theme, "So I can feel better/happier/more fulfilled." (We'll dig into the psychology of well-being in chapter 6. For now, let's take it to mean "satisfied with one's circumstances," including one's prospects.)

Next, ask what WHY means to them. Most unconsciously take an Aristotelian approach, trying to reason out their objectives with words.* Encouraged by workbooks, facilitators, and "experts," they use their experiences and intuition to try defining a single life goal.

Such assumptions form the backbone of what has become the *de*

---

* Revealingly, our word "logic" comes from the ancient Greek *logos*, meaning word, language, and reason.

facto standard approach to finding our WHY, which we'll explore in this chapter. Participants are invited to reflect upon their life experiences, motivations and work joys, to consult friends about what they seem most passionate about, then craft a statement that captures the essence of all this to guide their careers going forward.

Already, there are inherent tensions here. If our WHY resides in our deepest seat of emotion, how can we put words to it? Emotions are notoriously hard to articulate. Artists and philosophers have tried for centuries to explain what it means to feel love, for example. Therapy clients spend years trying to understand what they want and what's holding them back. The results are rarely satisfying.

The idea that individual purpose is "the reason we exist" is popular—indeed, dictionaries often cite "the reason for doing something" as their first definition. Many naturally gravitate toward this idea and begin developing elaborate theories whereby to boil our lives down to an elegant explanation or theme.

Most, however, struggle with this exercise, and are not immediately sure why. Their frustration can be intense, even to the point of tears.

Now, try something different in your imaginary workshop. Throw open the conversation. Tell participants to forget the dictionary and the methodology. Flip the question: Ask not where they might find their WHY, but how their WHY might find them.

We've seen rooms light up with such guidance. The focus shifts from personal history to potential; past references continue, of course, but now tied to hypotheses about how to feel better. Participants share why they love their industry, or not. Where they hope their careers might go. How they might find their path, through a variety of personal experiments and less planned experiences.

WHAT PURPOSE ORIGINALLY MEANT

Given how fundamental it seems, it may surprise that "purpose" only appeared in English 700 years ago. Does this mean we didn't have versions of the concept before? Hardly. Previous philosophers used terms such as the Latin *functionem* (function) and the Greek *telos* (aim) to talk about our place in the world.

Like any neologism, "purpose" added a new shade of meaning. Ancient words said little about where our goals or functions came from— these were supposed to be self-evident, largely from our social roles.

"Purpose" emerged from the French verb *proposer*, "to put forward." For someone to have a purpose, they had to be "put forward" by something or someone. Members of feudal societies found their life goals from the class into which they were born ("put forward" by God) or by the commands of those "put forward" as their lords and masters (also powered by God).

As the Middle Ages drew to a close, questions arose about where authority to put anyone forward for anything actually lay. Protestants challenged the Catholic Church's claims to know God's plan, suggesting a more reliable method was to talk to Him themselves.

Fast-forward to today. The relationship between purpose and faith remains strong. Two-thirds of American adults feel their life mission is determined by a divine force. The most popular purpose guide of all time (50 million copies sold, 85 translations) is pastor Rick Warren's *The Purpose-Driven Life*. Even nominally secular self-help books like Kipp's *Claim Your Power* often frame purpose as a "calling" from a "higher power."

In light of this centuries-old cultural connection, little surprise that even nonbelievers now find themselves drawn to phrases like "what I'm supposed to do" when talking about their WHY, even as they struggle to say who or what is doing the supposing. The logic is built into the word itself: We are using a knife to drive screws.

At the same time, many believers struggle to discover a satisfactory sense of purpose through prayer, or prayer-like reflection, alone. Might a differently elaborated understanding of WHY work better?

THE STANDARD APPROACH

Dictionaries typically define "purposefulness" objectively or intellectually: "the fact of having a useful purpose" (Oxford Learner's) or "the quality of knowing what you intend to do" (Cambridge Advanced Learner's).

Our workshop and coaching experience suggests it's more helpful to see purpose as a *subjective* feeling. Like happiness, we tend to think of it as a desirable state (in contrast to undesirable "aimlessness"). Also like happiness, however, most of us do not intuitively understand where the feeling comes from. When we have it, we generally don't ask about its origins. When we don't, we go looking for the ingredients that might produce it, assuming—again, like happiness—that while its principles may be universal, personal recipes will vary.

Add in the task of figuring out how our individual WHY intersects with those of the groups in which we live and work—as the communitarian philosopher Charles Taylor argues, our identity is shaped by our social roles—and the possible paths to discovering it become numerous and complex.

In this light, the appeal of today's most popular approach to finding WHY is evident. It's straightforward, memorable, and fast—qualities as attractive in self-help as in management.

Yet as we've seen, it has also proved frustrating. Most still don't feel purposeful at work (chapter 2). Many hunger for an alternative. Before we can offer one, however, it's helpful to note how the standard approach works, where it delivers, and where it seems to be spinning its wheels.*

1. Our core WHY

Each individual is said to have a single, unchanging WHY that develops in our emotional, operational brains, becomes fixed in our youth, and stays with us throughout our lives. We cannot have more than one. No logical or psychological evidence is given for this.

2. Why WHY matters

As the physical core of our nervous systems, WHY is said to be what we are most motivated and satisfied by. It is why others are

---

* The following describes the approach in *Find Your Why: A Practical Approach for Discovering Purpose for You and Your Team* (2017), by David Mead, Peter Docker and Simon Sinek.

motivated to work with us or buy from us.

This is said to be true for both individuals and companies. Individuals can only feel fulfilled by finding and living their WHY. Companies can only succeed and win customers by doing the same. Others care less about WHAT we are doing or selling than WHY we are doing or selling it.

3. Finding our individual WHY

We find our individual WHY by reflecting on our lives, recalling moments in which we felt most fulfilled, and talking to those who know us best.

The goal is to craft a WHY statement that takes the following form: My purpose is to do X so that Y happens (Y being the difference we make in the world).

4. Finding a collective WHY

Discovering a team or company WHY is a bottom-up process. Teams gather to share and discuss their individual WHY statements. Common themes point to a collective or "tribal" WHY, which is then rendered into a similarly formatted statement.

Team WHYs are nested logically within the greater WHYs of larger groups like departments and business units, and ultimately the WHY of the whole organization, which should align with the WHY of the organization's founder/s.

CHALLENGES

All this has the undeniable virtue of simplicity: If these assumptions hold, individual and team WHYs can be discovered in a matter of days, then last for life.

Yet it's not entirely clear that they do.

1. Our brains and conscious minds do not work linearly.

There's no biological evidence to suggest our emotional limbic brain somehow evolved before our rational neocortex. Biologists believe they developed together and work together. Even if they didn't, it's unclear how the "age" or physical centrality of the limbic brain would give it a logical upper hand in navigating life.

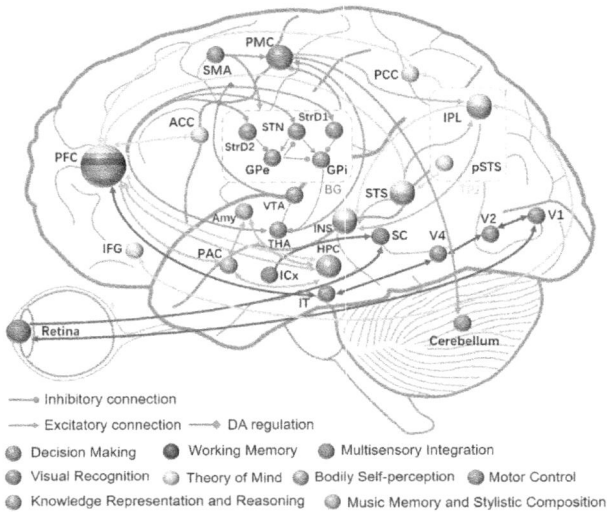

Exhibit 3.1: The physical interplay of cognitive functions
Source: Zhao Dongcheng

Neither our brains nor our minds operate in linear fashion. Various parts of the brain collaborate with our nervous systems to deliver conscious experience. They also do much that we are not conscious of. Electrical impulses move through us asynchronously and iteratively with some localization but no "center." Emotions sometimes seem to drive our thoughts, as when joy makes us more optimistic. Yet the reverse is also true: The thought of losing a thing or person we value triggers grief.

2. There's no reason to think we have only one purpose in life, nor that it is formed in our youth.

Like our brains, our life paths are nonlinear. We may have guesses in school about what we should do as adults. Some feel a "calling" to be doctors, teachers, or artists, for example. A subset might later feel they've guessed correctly, achieving an enduring sense of fulfillment.

Others will revisit their guesses as they live and learn. Even the post-secondary path followed by 62 percent of American high school graduates doesn't work for everyone: Two in five college freshmen drop out within six years. Beyond that, many (including this book's authors) discover they had no idea what their dream profession actually entails until they start work. Most college graduates change careers before they turn thirty, twice. After their first job experience, a third change *fields*.

This is healthy, according to career counselors. Our twenties are a good time to experiment, before our professional mobility becomes constrained by life commitments and work experience. Nor does learning through work stop then. In 2021, almost half of working people of all ages said they were considering a career change.

(*This Is Your Life, A Career and Education Planning Guide*, Government of Alberta, page 3)

Exhibit 3.2: Most career paths are nonlinear.
Source: Government of Alberta

Even if we've found our ideal job before we turn thirty-nine—the average age for a major change—there's no saying that it will be around for long. The world is always changing. Technological progress, evolving consumer preferences, business ups and downs—all these and more may make the thing we loved doing in our twenties and thirties redundant by the time we reach the prime earning years of our forties and fifties. AI may do to paralegals, software engineers, and others what previous technologies did to switchboard operators, movie projectionists and VCR repair technicians.

Individuals change as well. Artists who felt a calling in their teens may wake up years later wanting a steadier paycheck. Nurses and doctors may simply burn out, as did thousands during the pandemic.

Given all this, the prospects of forming a latent WHY in our teens that will last our whole lives are, at best, uncertain.

3. We're not that articulate.

The idea of a rousing statement that can act as an enduring guide to fulfillment may be appealing.

Even if this were theoretically possible, however, another hurdle exists: Most of us aren't wordsmiths.

A few may be able to articulate a life theme they find useful, through reflection, coaching, and effort. Yet many aren't so capable. We often struggle to write good emails. Even when they succeed, the product tends to be so generic that it is uninspiring or unhelpful ("I help people feel better," "I fix things," "I inspire others").

4. Nested WHYs are the exception.*

In the kind of seamless world that economists assume for simplicity, an organization's parts might fit together like machine components. Individual cogs would be in the right jobs, fitting together into larger mechanisms (teams and business units) that then deliver on the collective WHY.

If only the world worked that way.

Economist Alex Tabarrok notes that when relatively simple systems (like leadership teams) try to govern complex systems (like companies), they invariably produce unintended consequences. Most companies evolve without, or in spite of, conscious design. Original structures are added to and refined as opportunities and needs arise, often with unnoticed or unintended overlaps in roles. In the matrix structures of some larger companies, this overlap is even deliberate; corporate and geographic divisions are expected to hash out their differences. Furthermore, "reorging" remains an ongoing ritual among the Fortune 1000. New designs are often based not on hard data, but theories that need to be trialed and refined based on experience.

Individuals, meanwhile, are often ill-suited to or unhappy with their roles—Gallup recently pegged the US figure at 65 percent— having taken them out of necessity, gotten stuck mid-career, or seen

---

* This point gets into the question of collective WHYs, which are the subject of chapters 4 and 5. We address them here simply to follow the standard approach, and will refer back as necessary.

their roles reinvented. Responsibilities are not always well-defined. Overlaps arise accidentally. Disputes over authority abound. Teams at headquarters struggle to maintain a connection to customers, and any sense of collective purpose frays. To boot, the goals or purpose of founders, while often powerful, can fail to stand the test of time. New market demands, technologies, and leadership force pivots and reinventions.

These are not necessarily good or bad. American Express is no longer a mail delivery service. YouTube is no longer a dating website. Slack is not a chat service for gamers. This does not diminish the value each creates every day. Like individuals, companies are malleable entities that must adapt in an ever-changing world. They survive and provide lasting value not by sticking to foundational WHYs or requiring perpetual alignment but by experimenting, learning, and evolving their WHYs as needed.

None of this is to suggest that an organization of nested WHYs that align with individual WHYs is not a fine goal to work towards. It's just not something we can assume already exists, as WowCo discovered.

HOW WE ACTUALLY FEEL WHY

If we can't rely on our cultural intuitions and simplifying assumptions, what's left?

We've noticed two telling patterns.

First, as noted in our Preface, is how people talk differently about purpose in and out of workshops.

Offsites of any kind are, by their nature, artificial exercises: a step out of normal work and life to play a kind of game with goals most never think about, like team visions, and unfamiliar rules ("Let's work this out in a day!"). They have become standard practice for good reason, drawing out important ideas and concerns that might otherwise go unnoticed. They can also be misleading. Many feel the need to impress their bosses and peers by "winning" at the workshop game. If a question is asked, no matter how weird ("If we were an animal, what would we be?"), they want to give dazzling answers.

Playing within strange rules for articulating WHY, workshop participants often find their minds twisted into mental pretzels, making ingenious discoveries that will not survive the game's end. "We're really an *upgrade* company!" we heard an executive with an auto body repair chain declare to rapturous participant applause—until it became apparent, in the cold light of regular business, that they really weren't.

The second pattern is how the conversation changes when we move past cultural habits.

One way to do this to impose more constructive rules, such as asking participants to eliminate the passive voice ("This is what I'm meant to do"—meant by whom?), vagueness ("I want to impact something bigger than myself"—anything?), or declarations so high level they could apply to anyone ("My purpose is to make the world a better place"—isn't everybody's?).*

Another is to expand the playing field: Ask participants to attempt articulations on the day, but then to revisit these guesses days or weeks later, after there's been time to live with the first draft and think. What surfaces is a clearer sense of what we know, what we need to figure out, and how a period of mindfulness can help close the gap.

Given a narrower scope and time to reflect (and act), we've found workshop participants tend to think differently about WHY.

Purpose begins to show up less as a "reason for which something exists or is done," a dictate we must follow, than a kind of working theory of where we might feel impact.

And the very process of finding how to have impact starts to look itself like a goal, or WHY, in itself.

---

* Patrick Sheehan, a Stanford researcher interviewed on Jane Marie's *The Dream* podcast in 2023, observed that the WHY of most inspirational coaches, many of whom have chosen the profession after finding no inspiration in their own careers, is simply "to inspire."

WHAT WE REALLY WANT

Is feeling purposeful at work a goal in itself or a contribution to something else—like feeling happy in life?

Our work with teams has led us to suspect the latter, which we'll explore in more detail in chapter 6.

First, it's worth touching on what we know about feeling happy at work, which correlates highly with what has come to be called "engagement."

As companies have become increasingly focused on engagement, researchers have developed tools to help them understand it. One of the most widely used and revealing is Gallup's long-running Q12 Survey. Based on over 2 million responses collected since its 1998 inception, the Q12 identifies twelve factors correlated with engagement, from feeling one's opinions are valued to having a best friend at work. Like Maslow, Gallup has sorted these factors into a hierarchy, where higher needs only become a concern once basic ones have been satisfied.

Purpose only shows up explicitly in one of the statements respondents are asked to agree or disagree with: (8. "The mission or purpose of my company makes me feel my job is important."). Implicitly, however, the idea runs through almost the entire survey, shedding light on how WHY drives engagement. These employee needs are worth reviewing before we turn to those of companies.

Basic Needs

1. I know what is expected of me at work.
2. I have the materials and equipment I need to do my work right.

Note what isn't here, or anywhere in the Q12: compensation.

All things being equal, most of us would prefer to be paid more rather than less. Not simply because of the lifestyle and opportunities this affords, but as a measure of our personal value.

As Daniel Pink found in *Drive*, however, this is not necessarily the top thing we are looking for at work, particularly in certain types of jobs, as we'll see in chapter 9. We all want to be paid fairly. But many find themselves in the fortunate position of being able to find alternative positions with comparable compensation, and are, thus, willing to trade some amount of pay in exchange for work that's more meaningful and enjoyable.

Gallup Q^{12} Survey

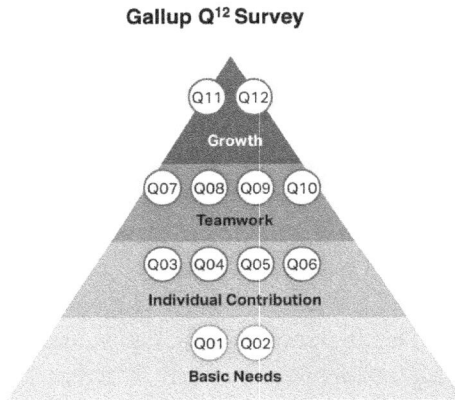

Exhibit 3.3: Gallup Q12 employee engagement survey
Source: Gallup

In certain cases, more pay can even be felt to devalue the intrinsic worth of the work itself. When a design firm we worked with began paying revenue-based bonuses to its creatives, engagement actually went down. The job started to seem less about innovation, creativity, and teamwork than delivering exactly what clients want.

Once we're okay with the paycheck, our most critical needs are the two listed above: to understand what our responsibilities are and to have the essential tools to do them. If your job is to sell and your company can't afford to develop or produce products, you'll only hurt yourself by sticking around.

Individual Contribution

3. At work, I have the opportunity to do what I do best every day.
4. In the last seven days, I have received recognition or praise for doing good work.

5. My supervisor, or someone else at work, seems to care about me as a person.

6. There is someone at work who encourages my development.

This is where purpose begins to show up. If the WHY we seek is a feeling of impact, clearly we need to be able to have impact (3) and get feedback (4) to indicate that. This can come from multiple sources, but even an overjoyed customer is not as meaningful as an approving manager or colleague (5).

The feeling and confidence that we are developing our abilities is a measure of our potential impact (6). This isn't just a matter of appreciation; we also need enough rope to do more.

Inevitably, our supervisor's opinion trumps all. The single most reported driver of workplace misery is a bad boss; half of us will leave a job at some point to escape one. As the saying goes, people join companies and quit managers. They can also disengage.

Teamwork

7. At work, my opinions seem to count.

8. The mission or purpose of my company makes me feel my job is important.

9. My associates or fellow employees are committed to quality work.

10. I have a best friend at work.

Human beings have evolved to be social animals, as we'll explore in chapter 6. Up to 50 percent of the population requires human interaction some of the time, even introverts.

Much of this is satisfied in our lives outside of work. Still, we spend almost half of our waking hours with coworkers. In our thirties and forties, work becomes our main source of new friendships. Companies are a prime source of company.

This is why it matters that we connect with our coworkers (10) and have a voice (7). We need them to be committed to more than just kidding around while we wait for the quitting-time whistle to blow. For our work to matter, our team's work has to matter (8 and 9).

Growth

11. In the last six months, someone at work has talked to me about my progress.

    12. This last year, I have had opportunities at work to learn and grow.

    These build upon (6), where there's someone who encourages our development at work. We want our work to have a dual impact: on the organization and on ourselves.

⚷

All told, these drivers form a compelling, insightful, data-driven picture of what employees need at work. Employers will seek to satisfy them if they want their people to be happy and to perform.

    But what do employees actually need them to do? ⚷

KEY TAKEAWAYS

1. Despite all the interest in purpose and WHY, it has not been clearly defined by those discussing it—and it's not entirely clear what we're looking for because of this.

2. Popular approaches to purpose include several common but unsupported assumptions about how it works:
   a. Purpose is a singular, lifelong feature of each personality formed in our early years;
   b. It operates linearly in our brains and can manifest itself accordingly in our work;
   c. It's readily discoverable through exercises; and
   d. It can be pieced together with others' to create a collective WHY.

3. These assumptions leave workshop participants frustrated because:
   a. There's no scientific basis or evidence that we have a singular, linear WHY that forms in our youth.
   b. The exercise of finding that singular WHY requires us to be more articulate than we actually are.
   c. The standard process of finding our WHY does not align with how teams actually form and work together in companies.

4. In our work, we've found that WHY is actually:
   a. More like a feeling, which is hard to articulate,
   b. Something we discover in stages,
   c. Something that changes throughout our lives, and
   d. Something that operates at two levels, where the search itself is part of our purpose.

5. For employees, WHY is closely related to our sense of engagement or connection to our work and manifests itself through twelve factors that Gallup has identified in its long-running Q12 survey.

CHAPTER 4

What Companies Do

"Profit is what happens when you do everything else right."

YVON CHOUINARD

YOUR AUTHORS ENTERED THE BUSINESS WORLD at a disadvantage. We were exotics, senior-level hires without business degrees and didn't know the lingo.

A particularly challenging term was "value creation."

At a training session for new hires, a Boston Consulting Group partner asked the room what the phrase meant.

Hands shot up. (Not ours.)

"TSR," said a newly minted MBA. Heads nodded approvingly, including the partner's.

We stared at each other blankly. (TSR stands for "Total Shareholder Return," the value companies deliver to owners through dividends and rising stock prices.)

Afterward, the exotics compared notes. Surely, there had to be more to value creation than TSR. Where did those dividends and that share price growth come from?

Little did we know that at that moment, three thousand miles away, a McKinsey Global Institute Fellow was working on that very question—nor that his answer would eventually fill a five-hundred-page book.

HOW WE ALL PROFIT FROM PROFIT

Before digging into the purpose of companies, let's start with the basic assumption: They want to make money.

Profit, as we've seen, sits at the core of Milton Friedman's famous doctrine (chapter 1). "There is one and only one social responsibility of business," it stipulates:

> *To use its resources and engage in activities designed to increase its profits so long as it stays within the rules of the game: open and free competition without deception or fraud.*

How pursuing profit legitimately might have any kind of social impact—let alone be a social responsibility—may not be immediately obvious. To understand how creating shareholder value might entail creating social value, a brief crash course in microeconomics is warranted.*

Exhibit 5.1 depicts the basic paradigm upon which modern economics is founded: markets work according to supply and demand. The key elements for our purposes are the highlighted fields labeled "surplus." To understand what these represent, we need to understand the lines that define them.

The line marked S represents the quantity of products (Q) that producers are willing to supply at various price points (P); the higher the price, the more producers are willing to supply. The line marked D represents the quantity buyers are willing to buy at various prices. For them, it goes the opposite way: The lower the price, the more they will buy.

What's relatively easy to grasp here is how producers create value

---

* If you're already versed in the subject, feel free to skip this section. If this isn't enough, check out the Khan Academy's great tutorials.

for themselves by selling goods and services for more than they cost to deliver, which is the "profit." These numbers are easy to track and show up in financial statements. Total all the profit made in a given period, and you get what economists call "producer surplus," shown in the lower shaded triangle.

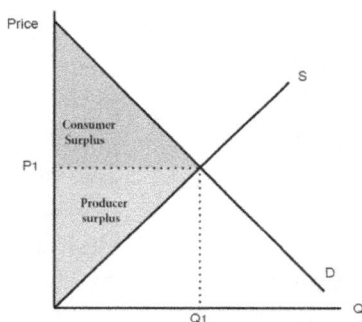

Exhibit 4.1: Supply and demand curves
Source: Economics Helps

So far, so good. Less familiar to most, however—and the essential piece for us—is the other kind of value generated: among buyers.

The upper triangle shows the difference between what each would be willing to pay for a product, and the market price (a bit like the difference between how much cash fans bring to a concert for scalpers' tickets and how much they actually have to pay to get in). The money buyers collectively save is their logical equivalent of profit: hence, "consumer surplus."

This is what Friedman and like-minded economists take to be the primary social good companies create. Firms' conscious objective may be their own profit triangle, but they all but inevitably create what we might call "consumer profit."*

The biggest challenge when it comes to understanding and valuing this good is that there's no real way to measure it. Consumers

---

* Exceptions occur when a company has a lot of market power, like a monopoly. Learn more with one of the Khan Academy tutorials.

don't generally think about the maximum they're willing to pay until they actually have to bite the bullet and pay it. Few track all the money they save from better prices, especially if they turn around and spend it on something else—and giving credit to companies that collectively made such prices possible is hardly a natural intuition.

The social benefits of companies trying to make money don't stop here. Producers have to do something with their profits. They can save it or distribute it to shareholders, in both cases increasing the supply of money (thus lowering borrowing rates) that others can use to create businesses and buy things like houses. Or firms can invest it in their own growth, creating more consumer profit in the future. Whatever they do, short of burying the money in the ground, profitable companies can't help but deliver broader value into the economy, including creating jobs and paying wages. This, in turn, creates more consumer demand and surpluses in the future.

For Friedmanites, there are only two ways a company can do all of the above *and* cause social harm. One is by defrauding customers: misrepresenting the value of their product. The other is by polluting: creating by-product waste that harms third parties.*

To increase their collective impact, honest, nonpolluting firms need to do one of two things, both of which we've seen Peter Drucker call out (chapter 2). They can attract more customers, shifting the demand curve (D) up: what Drucker calls "marketing" or "creating a customer." Or they can become more efficient, shifting the supply curve down, which Drucker calls "innovation." (Innovating new features can also increase what customers are willing to pay, raising demand.) All of this grows both triangles, including consumer surplus.

All this seems straightforward enough, but it's still based on a lot of assumptions: notably, that producers and consumers already agree what products might have value.

How does that happen?

---

* Some have argued for a third category—selling products that actually hurt the customer, like tobacco or unhealthy foods—though purists argue this is just a variant of the first two.

HOW IS VALUE ACTUALLY CREATED?

Many economists see their job as applying more specific, realistic assumptions to these radically simplified models—conditions that might lead suppliers to produce a loss, for example, as most start-ups do.

Many economists, but not all. In the 1950s, a Romanian Cold War refugee-turned-Vanderbilt economist came to believe that the above paradigm has a blind spot.

So focused had the field become on how markets acted within themselves, noted Nicholas Georgescu-Roegen, that that they overlooked how markets came to exist in the first place.

Such elegant models were fine so long as one only thought about a market as a self-contained, closed system. But this was to ride roughshod over critical questions about value creation:

- How did producers and buyers find each other?
- How did producers learn what customers would pay for, what inputs were required to deliver, and whether this could be done profitably and sustainably?
- What exactly *was* waste? What effect did undesirable by-products have on consumers and third parties, that is, society? How did this impact other markets?

Georgescu-Roegen took a broader view—much broader. All economic activity, he observed, was fundamentally a physical reordering of things. Companies acquired and blended natural resources with labor to produce goods, services, and waste.

The rub? Not all reordering delivered value. Some activities, like selling hard drugs or holding loud outdoor concerts, might actually create more harm than good to customers and third parties. *True* value was only created by reducing disorder that cost time and money to manage, thus making human life easier and better.

This argument remained relatively obscure beyond academic circles until it caught the attention of Eric Beinhocker, the McKinsey Fellow mentioned at the outset of this chapter. His 2006 tome, *The Origin of Wealth*, aimed to explain an economic miracle: how industrialization had delivered an almost 13,000 percent increase in humanity's annual value creation, through increases in population and output per capita.

Beinhocker built on Georgescu-Roegen's principles, zeroing in on their implications over time. Each act of value creation or positive reordering increased our species' cumulative know-how, freeing us up to focus on solving new problems.

Consider the example of bringing fresh water to a community that previously had to fetch it on foot. All the hours of a day saved by turning a tap rather than going to the well? This was time that could now be allocated to other value-creating activities—such as bringing pipes into individual homes, which would free up even more time. Such innovation would also create new needs—in this case, for plumbing services—creating more jobs, more knowledge and new demands, i.e., for plumbing tools.

For Beinhocker, this insight cracked the nut on how value creation really happens. "Wealth is knowledge," he concluded. "Prosperity in a society is the accumulation of solutions to human problems."

Which still left a nagging question. How did we develop such useful knowledge, like the know-how to manufacture and lay pipe and, well, plumb? Beinhocker saw the processes of seeking profit, competition, and innovation as fundamentally analogous to the principles of evolution: "Differentiate, select, and amplify." Changing our environment did not put an end to what biologist Charles Darwin called natural selection. It merely shifted the venue from human genetic adaptation to adapting our environment to us, which we do every day.

The Prussian general and author Carl von Clausewitz once called war "the continuation of policy by other means." Likewise, in light of the preceding arguments, we might reasonably say business is the continuation of science by other means.

Hold that thought—we shall return to it in chapter 6.

THE PRODUCTIVITY IMPERATIVE

Georgescu-Roegen's and Beinhocker's insights are not at odds with Friedman's, who spent his later years underlining the pollution problem to anyone who listened (notably in a famous 1979 appearance on *The Phil Donahue Show*). But they shed new light on the WHY of companies. Firms don't just produce profit with consumer surplus as a happy side effect. They reorder the parts of the world in ways that address human needs, whatever the scale: from a pharma company whose vaccine saves millions of lives to a neighborhood bodega that allows customers to avoid the drive to a big store.

Let's connect this to our investigation so far.

Ask any economist, policymaker, or business leader for the single most important measure of economic progress and you're likely to get the same answer: productivity growth, as we saw in chapter 1. To understand what companies actually do to deliver this, however, we must dig a bit farther.

First, let's recap the benefits of productivity growth. When employees are able to produce more stuff or deliver greater service with the same effort, their value goes up. Wages and incomes rise, even if they don't always keep pace—a problem we'll return to in chapter 9. Businesses grow and create jobs. All this drives demand and raises living standards.* Moreover, the benefits don't get trapped within a given economy. The wealthier a country gets, the more it imports from poorer ones, creating jobs and raising incomes there as well.†

Next, growth in productivity drives international competitiveness (as new products and methods are imitated) which increases global consumer surplus along the same lines. Companies are able to sell more abroad at better prices.

---

* The distribution of benefits may not be equitable, as many reasonably object.

† Caveat: If these jobs are offshored, as many manufacturing jobs in developed economies have been, displaced workers aren't always able to find jobs with comparable compensation. This creates real pain, but it also creates jobs and growth overseas.

Third, it drives further innovation. Greater efficiency in one area creates opportunity to focus on others.

Last, and controversially, it should drive environmental sustainability. The first versions of a production process tend to be wasteful. Early-stage firms often lack the resources to dispose of such waste responsibly. Greater productivity makes more responsible environmental practices more affordable—though actually pursuing them typically requires social and political pressure.

This all sounds good. So what's the problem?

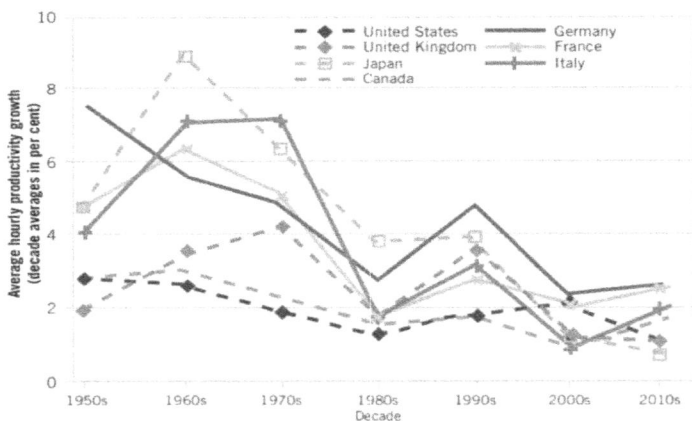

Source: Penn World Tables version 9, available at: https://www.rug.nl/ggdc/productivity/pwt/, authors' calculations.

Exhibit 4.2: G7 productivity growth by country, 1950–2015.
Source: Ekkehard Ernst, Rossana Merola, Daniel Saaman

All things being equal—that is, setting aside relatively rare circumstances such as wars, financial crises, and the arrival of a generationally disruptive technology—economists would expect productivity growth to climb steadily. If each generation of solutions adds to our stock of knowledge, what we're able to do with that knowledge should increase, right?

As we've seen, things haven't quite worked out that way since Robert Solow first made the case (chapter 1). US productivity growth has been falling since the 1960s. In the first half of 2022, nonfarm productivity fell at an unprecedented annualized rate of 6 percent. Other industrialized countries have seen higher highs and lower lows (Exhibit 4.2). Real wage growth has slowed even further, lagging behind productivity growth in the US by 2 percent annually since 1979 (Exhibit 1.2) and even more elsewhere (3 percent in the UK, for example).

The jury's out on what's driving this decline. Suspects include a failure to keep improving the use of new technologies, the aging workforce (we're more motivated to innovate earlier in our careers, when we expect to reap the rewards), declining R&D investment, and more. The decline in real wage growth appears related to global workforce competition, pressuring the value of unskilled labor, widening the gap between white- and blue-collar compensation, and creating economically harmful social divisions.*

Whatever the causes or prospects for policy-driven solutions, frontline responsibility for reversing these trends rests in the hands of our central institutions of knowledge and wealth creation: companies. Many of the above factors influencing productivity growth may be beyond the control of individual firms. But one remains squarely within it, even if policymakers rarely pay it much heed: the fact that so few feel sufficiently engaged at work to put in more than minimum effort.

Here, there is much work to do. And only companies can do it. ⌐

---

* For more on these trends and their prospects, see chapter 9.

KEY TAKEAWAYS   ⚷

1. Companies' primary purpose is to create value for shareholders, in the form of share price increases and dividends, but how do they actually create value day-to-day, for both shareholders and stakeholders?

2. In creating microeconomics' supply/demand paradigm, economist Alfred Marshall showed how companies in competitive markets create an equivalent to profit for buyers called "consumer surplus."

3. Consumer surplus is the money buyers save compared to what they were willing to pay—savings they can then use to purchase other products and services, in turn driving demand and financing other businesses.

4. The widespread benefit of this consumer surplus makes businesses question how they might create the things that buyers want at lower prices.

5. Economist Nicholas Georgescu-Roegen saw economic activity as transformations of the physical world that reduce disorder and serve human needs.

6. McKinsey's Eric Beinhocker built on this concept to explain how value builds over time, declaring that "prosperity...is the accumulation of solutions to human problems" and "wealth is knowledge."

7. Since we're always accumulating knowledge, productivity growth (better ways of doing things) should be trending upwards—and yet it is falling, leaving us to wonder, What's missing?

8. Many factors economists point to in this devastating decline are beyond firms' control, but not to one that's emerging as a leading suspect: engagement. Here, companies have work to do.

CHAPTER 5

What Companies Need

"Profit is the reward for correctly understanding an aspect of reality ahead of your peers."

ALAIN DE BOTTON

HOW CAN COMPANIES GET BETTER at what they want to do (making money) and what society needs them do to (solving human problems)? How can they better organize how knowledge is created and processed? What does this have to do with engagement and purpose?

The Purpose Gap surfaced by McKinsey, along with complementary findings from other researchers (chapter 2), suggests that different parts of organizations have competing views not just about *what* they're supposed to be doing (their WHY) but *how* to do it.

As leaders around the world have learned to their chagrin, these cannot be talked into alignment. Leaders need to grasp the intersection of what companies and employees want and how the day-to-day work environment affects both.

WHAT DO COMPANIES DO ALL DAY?

Richard Scarry's 1968 children's book *What Do People Do All Day?* taught preschoolers about the mysterious things adults do when they leave the house. In whimsical panoramas, Scarry illustrated how individuals from farmers to construction workers sometimes work alone, and sometimes in groups called companies.

Curiously, it took grown-ups far longer than one might expect to wonder about what drives this distinction. After the legal scholar Adam Smith effectively created modern economics in the 1770s, economists spent one and a half centuries talking about the behavior of firms without ever stopping to ask why they even exist.

The question is not as odd or a as it might seem. After all, we long managed to get by without companies. For most of our journey as a species, human beings produced and exchanged goods and services through ad hoc collaboration. As we saw in chapter 2, the birth of the modern corporation as a legal construct was driven largely by special historical circumstances, notably the need for a vehicle to finance overseas ventures. Even then, informed observers like Lord Thurlow doubted we had the design right. This curious legal artifice took center stage in Europe during the Industrial Revolution, thrived during the ensuing explosion of value creation discussed in chapter 4, and never really left. The institution of the company, in various flavors, now sits at the core of economies all around the world. While the rise of crowdwork companies like Uber and Upwork has challenged assumptions about the viability of economies based on self-employment, there's no question of returning to a pre-corporate world that effectivel operated as one big gig economy.

This alone should tell us something about firms' necessary, practical purpose. But what?

⌐━

In 1937, a young London School of Economics lecturer took it upon himself to provide an answer.

The paper in which he did so was short—less than 7,000 words, roughly a third of today's average—and so plainly argued that the author himself later dismissed it as "little more than an undergraduate essay."

For most of Ronald Coase's distinguished career, the world appeared to agree with his self-assessment. In the half century after its publication, "The Nature of the Firm" garnered a respectable but hardly earth-shaking 2,000 citations.

The next three decades, however, saw it receive more than 45,000.

The watershed was Coase's 1991 receipt of the Nobel Prize in Economics, which revealed as much about contemporary preoccupations as his ideas' timeless value. As we saw in chapter 2, late twentieth century managers and observers were growing increasingly curious about the purpose of the company and its role as our primary economic institution.

The genius of Coase's explanation lies in its simplicity: Corporations lower transaction costs. Or, as information economists like Friedrich Hayek put it, they organize and process useful knowledge.

Let's unpack this.

Every product that comes into our lives does so through a series of value-adding steps. Take french fries. Someone needs to acquire land, equipment, seed segments, water, know-how, and labor so that potatoes can be planted, grown, and harvested. Someone needs to drive them to a factory for processing. There they must be sliced, frozen, and packaged as a brand so consumers can find them before being delivered to a store. They then need to be displayed, sold, and taken home or delivered.

It's possible for one vertically integrated enterprise to handle most if not all these steps. The world's largest french fry manufacturer, McCain Foods, not only manages brands in the frozen food aisle. It also owns proprietary DNA sequences that help its potatoes grow larger and faster, with less risk of blight. In short, it has expanded up and down the value chain— hence, "vertically."

Still, it's not necessary for such a broad array of functions to live under one roof. Coase recognized how such steps can be performed by different entities, even individuals. Many food companies sell products grown by independent farmers, transported by independent drivers, and so on. Indeed, this is how most goods are produced today. Apple designs and sells its electronics directly to consumers. But it does not own the overseas factories that build them, nor the ships that transport them, nor many third-party retail outlets, from Amazon to Walmart, that also sell them.

Why own some parts of the value chain but not others? This is the question Coase sought to answer. His solution turns on seeing the moves between steps as transactions: The output of one must be transferred as an input to the next. Each transaction has costs, including searching for a supplier or purchaser, communicating with them, negotiating terms, coordinating transfer, and so on. When such costs are high, it can make sense to reduce them by bringing them under common control.

Costs go up when information about other steps is low, and the risks of error or delay high. Firms are thus knowledge centers, places where information can be used more efficiently, transaction costs lowered, and proprietary know-how accumulated. For Coase's admirers, which arguably includes most microeconomists, a firm's boundaries are defined by what it chooses to insource or outsource, effectively defining its core business. Standardized, easily replicable steps like office cleaning or the hosting of computing power, can be outsourced, unless those are the firm's business. The same holds true for more complex processes that may not be needed regularly, such as legal or consulting advice. Only the most complex, uncertain, and differentiated processes, like sourcing the tastiest potatoes or managing a brand, get organized inside a company.

At first, this may seem like just another theory, comparable to the "big pictures" mapped out by Friedman and Georgescu-Roegen. Look more closely, however, and a key difference emerges—one so critical that it makes Coase's theory of the firm, as the Nobel committee noted, a truly practical touchpoint for managers. Unlike other models, its perspective is essentially bottom up, focused not on market outcomes but day-to-day managerial decisions.

Patagonia founder Yvon Chouinard once observed, "profit is the effect of doing everything else right." Coase's model tells us specifically what "everything else" means: accumulating knowledge that reduces transaction costs in order to deliver better products to the right buyers. Company-specific production and marketing formulas, what managers sometimes call their "secret sauce," is their essential source of competitive advantage, much of it living in the heads of their people.

As we've seen, this insight has been restated in other terms by management giants. Peter Drucker called it "creating and keeping a customer," the result of "two and only two functions: marketing and innovation." Sequoia's Don Valentine calls it "achieving product-market fit." For management theorist Alain de Botton, it's "discovering an aspect of reality before your peers."

But how do companies do this sustainably? What is the role of teams? In Kōnosuke Matsushita's terms (chapter 2), how do bosses get out of their own heads and into employees'?

To answer that, we must go even farther back in the history of modern economics and management—in fact, to its origin.

WHY WE NEED PURPOSE AT WORK

Adam Smith sealed his place in history with a 1776 book that touched only tangentially on his core expertise as a jurist, but would come to be seen as the foundation of modern economics. *On the Origins and Causes of the Wealth of Nations* (commonly known as *The Wealth of Nations*) was an immediate hit, going through four editions and multiple translations before Smith's death in 1791, and two more before the century was out.

Less well-known is the work that made Smith a celebrity decades earlier. His 1759 debut, *The Theory of Moral Sentiments*, sold almost as well as *The Wealth of Nations* during his lifetime. It fell into an Enlightenment genre known as "moral philosophy," a blend of what we now call psychology (how emotions and thoughts work) and self-help (what we must do to be happy).

Economists and business audiences since have naturally gravitated toward the later book, which sheds a still-compelling light on the ways domestic markets create value and international markets distribute it. *Sentiments*'s citations have outpaced *Wealth*'s by an order of magnitude. Close readers, however, have never forgotten the preface to the latter's third edition, which positioned the earlier work as an essential "preliminary." Why? Because it was impossible to understand why human beings make great market participants—including why their uncoordinated efforts produce a favorable distribution of things "as if by an invisible hand"—without grasping human psychology.

Smith's explanation of why human markets work rests on two claims. First is that we get intrinsic pleasure from serving others, as long as such service doesn't clash with our own interests. "How selfish soever man may be supposed," ran *Sentiments*'s opening line,

> *there are evidently some principles in his nature, which interest him in the fortune of others, and render their happiness necessary to him, though he derives nothing from it except the pleasure of seeing it.*

His second claim was related: that we have a capacity for what he called "sympathy" and what we now call cognitive empathy.* Humans are able to imagine what might make others feel happier. We take our perspectives on our own wants and needs, together with our experiences of what tends to satisfy them, to develop solutions that might satisfy others.

By way of illustration, take a favorite example of Smith's contemporaries. To attract customers, a would-be innkeeper first needs to acquire property located where she imagines travelers might want to stop for the night. She needs to figure out how they will find it,

---

* Smith did not use the word "empathy" anywhere in his writings, as it did not exist until the early twentieth century. He used the word "sympathy." What he meant, however—the ability to project ourselves into others' situations—is what most psychologists now call "cognitive empathy." See the Preface for a more detailed discussion about the types of empathy.

say through signage or word of mouth. She needs to see the place through their eyes: Does it look appealing? What might induce them to choose her inn over those of her competitors? Does the smell of delicious food work? Or does she need a bar where they can have a drink and be persuaded to stay?

This kind of empathy is not benevolence or compassion. It's simply an imaginative ability, also used in anticipating an adversary's moves in war, negotiating a deal, or even committing fraud.* Smith and his peers were fascinated by the outward similarity between such self-interested activity in legitimate market activity—the innkeeper's main concern, after all, is to make money—and the other-regarding love the Bible's Golden Rule called for: doing unto others as you would have them do unto you. The implication? Self-interested economic behavior could lead to social peace.

Alas, Smith's insights on market psychology did not extend to the workplace. He celebrated the productivity benefits of the "division of labor"—having workers specialize on simple steps in manufacturing processes along a production line—without a second thought for the psychic toll such narrowness might exact.

We can now appreciate how the twenty-first century thought leaders we met in chapter 2 effectively built upon Smith's notion that producers need empathy to anticipate customer needs, by recognizing that most purchasing decisions have an emotional dimension. Customers don't just care about a product's features, but about how it makes them feel.

This meshes with what we've discovered in the last chapter and this one about the universal WHY of firms: to solve human problems in ever better ways by accumulating know-how and reducing costs. To do so sustainably, companies need to combine the power of existing know-how and assets with fresh insight into customer needs and process efficiency, which comes from the cognitive empathy of its people.

Empathy's essential, catalyzing role has won growing recognition

---

* Industrial psychologists have noted that con artists and sociopaths require high degrees of cognitive empathy to manipulate their prey.

among leaders. Microsoft CEO Satya Nadella has made it his mantra, celebrating it as "the core of innovation" (the only way to anticipate customer needs) as well as leadership (understanding team needs). Not only is empathy not a "soft skill", he says:

> *it's the hardest skill we learn—to relate to the world, to relate to people that matter the most to us. Business purpose lives at the intersection of existing corporate assets and living human capability. Its task is not simply to make workers feel valued but to leverage their efforts into innovation and marketing. In short, it operationalizes empathy.*

Sounds great. How does this work in practice?

HOW PURPOSE SHOWS UP: THE "MAGIC THREE" VALUE DRIVERS

We will explore a management program for turning purpose into performance in chapter 8, after first considering the employee perspective (chapters 6 and 7).

Before doing so, it's helpful to outline the Magic Three value drivers, factors that purpose impacts and which in turn have tangible impact on productivity.

1. Fit

No one knows better than HR managers how costly it can be to hire the wrong people: individuals who are not interested in working as hard as their colleagues, for example; or won't respect the company's norms regarding, say, work-life balance; or are focused on their careers at the expense of others'. When racing to ship minimum viable products, a start-up can't have a perfectionist developer who refuses to release code.

"Fit" is a widely misunderstood term. It does not mean all thinking the same way nor coming to the table with like skills and experiences. Lack of diversity in these respects risks groupthink, blind spots, and low creativity. "If you always have the same ideas as me," we once heard a CEO say, "one of us is redundant."

The fit managers must aim for complementarity of work style and values. Teams don't need to agree on solutions or even problems. They must agree on how to approach them. A colleague who feels the need to constantly debate first principles belongs elsewhere.*

2. Alignment

Team values don't change with business cycles, project demands, or anything else.

Priorities, however, do. Alignment refers to the direction, prioritization, and synchronization of a team's efforts around deliverables at a given time.

Is a food company's new offering going to be a healthy snack, a guilty pleasure consumed in moderation, or something deliberately addictive? A product team that can't agree will find itself at cross-purposes, and may fail to produce a viable product.

Alignment is when all parts of a team or organization navigate by the same North Star. Nothing reduces productivity and engagement like an individual or subgroup focused on a project whose goals differ from the whole. Unchecked, such toxicity can spread like a disease (as we'll see in chapter 8)

3. Engagement

We've already discussed this last purpose-to-productivity driver, but here's our favorite definition:

> Employee engagement is the extent to which employees feel passionate about their jobs, are committed to the organization, and put discretionary effort into their work.

---

* Even a Ponzi scheme, as someone once joked in one of our workshops, needs its people to share its principles. If the overarching goal is to defraud investors, an employee who insists on telling the truth will undermine the whole enterprise.

Engagement is closely related to the other two drivers. As we've seen, however, it may be the most consequential: without "discretionary effort," going above and beyond the minimum required to do a job, it's almost impossible to raise productivity.

It's also the most elusive.

Keep the Magic Three in mind as we delve into the frontline manager's perspective on how to get purpose to work its magic. First, however, we must consider what they feel like from an employee perspective— what employees require to feel what they need to feel.

KEY TAKEAWAYS

1. It's one thing to understand in theory that the purpose of companies is to solve problems and create useful knowledge—it's another to grasp what this means on a daily basis.

2. In a Nobel Prize-winning paper, economist Ronald Coase identified a practical rationale for the existence of companies by focusing on how company officers determine what they should do as their core business versus what they should outsource.

3. Coase's answer was that companies should seek to minimize the transaction costs between steps of production processes: the steps a company understands best they do themselves, thus becoming a center of knowledge creation and deployment.

4. The human/employee element in this process starts with our ability to guess or understand what customers need, which is a display of empathy. Adam Smith saw it as the psychological foundation of all markets.

5. This is the understanding that has come to the fore of modern management: purchasing decisions are driven by emotional needs and employees use empathy to serve those needs. This includes understanding the needs of those they work with upstream and downstream in the production process.

6. Business purpose is at its root a tool for operationalizing empathy around a company's existing know-how and assets to gain new insights and solve problems.

7. Purpose in a company works primarily to impact the Magic Three value drivers:
    a. Fit: complementarity of work style and principles
    b. Alignment: agreement on goals, priorities, and pacing
    c. Engagement: connection with the organization and application of discretionary effort.

CHAPTER 6

What Employees Need

"Employees who believe that management is concerned about them as a whole person—not just an employee—are more productive, more satisfied, more fulfilled. Satisfied employees mean satisfied customers, which leads to profitability."

ANNE MULCAHY

FEW ADMIRERS OF ABRAHAM MASLOW'S hierarchy of needs realize he did not always admire it himself, and revised it to include insights with a longer and deeper history.

His original 1943 version had five levels. Human beings' ideal state, after achieving physical security and social status, was "self-actualization": realizing our full individual potential.

In the 1960s, Maslow moved to California and became immersed in the counterculture. Along with other psychologists, including LSD advocate Timothy Leary, he became a leading figure in the "human potential movement" that sought to better understand our "highest state."

Maslow came to believe he'd missed some steps. Shortly before his death in 1970, he added two more levels to the original five, above "esteem" and below "self-actualization": "cognitive needs" (understanding how things work) and "aesthetic needs" (living in beauty) (see Exhibit 6.1).

More significant was a change he'd made a few years earlier. Self-actualization isn't the true pinnacle of human experience, Maslow decided. Once we realize our personal potential, we go beyond our self to a closer connection with the universe—or what Maslow called "transcendence."

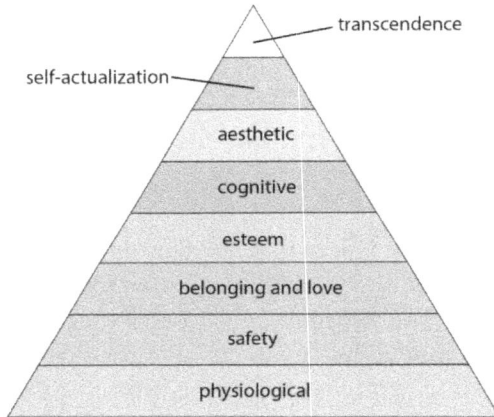

Exhibit 6.1: Maslow's final Hierarchy of Needs (1970)
Source: Simply Psychology

This was not an original discovery. For millennia, philosophers the world over have held that the ideal state of mental and spiritual fulfillment entails a liberation from self-concern and a connection with the universe to which they've given various names, from Hindu *moksha* and Greek *eudaimonia* to Christian grace and Zen *satori*.

Thirty years later, psychiatrist Martin Seligman named the discipline Maslow had effectively originated "positive psychology," since it focused less on remediating deficiencies than achieving growth. In the twenty-first century, the discipline morphed into what we now call "the science of happiness" or "the science of well-being."

To understand what employees really need from work, we must grasp this field's insights.

THE WHY OF WELL-BEING

The science of happiness has its critics. Well-being is so complex and subjective, they argue, that it cannot be measured or subject to true "scientific" study.

Tell that to the army of respected researchers at leading institutions, from Berkeley to Yale, who have surveyed thousands and attracted millions to their work through Massive Open Online Courses (MOOCs)—or Gallup, whose well-being indices have become some of its most popular products.

Some happiness researchers investigate external drivers of the state, like birth order and education level. More actionable studies zero in on the behaviors happy people practice, suggesting prescriptions for achieving a sense of well-being, whoever you may be.

While the details of the latter vary, three common ingredients have emerged:

1. Health

Our physical bodies are filters that shape our realities. We cannot be well if they are not. We need to get enough sleep and exercise, eat the right foods in reasonable amounts, and not ingest too many harmful substances.

Some also require meditation, other cognitive exercises, or particular supplements to aid well-being, such as medication.

Self-care alone will not make us happy. But it is a critical first step. As in-flight safety procedures demand, we must secure our own mask before assisting others, healthwise.

2. Gratitude

Just as we cannot breathe in and out simultaneously, it's all but impossible to feel thankful and deprived at the same time. The more we take stock of our blessings, the harder it is to feel regretful or resentful about things we don't have.

Inspired by Maslow's last revisions, some suggest that a better understanding of the world is itself a form of gratitude. The most popular definition of the word "appreciate" is "to recognize the worth of something," which requires understanding. The more we understand or "appreciate" about the world and others around us, the more we can feel grateful for it and them—and the better we feel ourselves.

3. Giving

As beings with biological needs, from food and shelter to rest and recreation, we must all take from the world.

Take too much, however, become selfish and self-absorbed, and happiness becomes all but impossible.

Self-care well above basic needs is a high-risk strategy, researchers argue, akin to placing all our chips on one square at the roulette table—a square labeled "me."

Care about what happens to other squares, however, and the odds of feeling better go up. Not only is "a joy shared a joy doubled," as Enlightenment philosopher Johann Wolfgang von Goethe observed. When we start to care about others, give to them, and promote their welfare, the game takes on a new dimension. When a person you staked or advised to bet on a given roulette square wins, you get a feeling of reward yourself ("I made that happen!").

This sounds a lot like what we heard from employees and managers in chapters 1 and 3, for whom feeling purposeful comes from having an impact on others.

Giving, aka impact, stands out from health and gratitude in two ways.

First, it's scalable. We can only be so healthy or feel so much gratitude. But there is no limit to the number of people we might impact, especially with the availability of mass channels.

Second, we can make a living from having impact.

Put these together and it becomes clear work is not simply an important place for feeling purposeful but happy as well.

OUR EVOLUTIONARY NEED FOR PURPOSE

After declaring that "wealth is knowledge" in *The Origin of Wealth,*

Eric Beinhocker adds, "Its origin is evolution."

By this he means we find solutions to human problems through a natural learning process that mimics the "trial, error, success and reproduction" dynamic Darwin saw as the essence of natural selection.

Is that just an analogy? Or do the similarities between evolution and learning run deeper?

A decade before Yuval Noah Harari culled insights from humanity's origins in 2014's *Sapiens*, sports journalist Christopher McDougall set out on a less ambitious quest: to find the perfect running shoe. His journey led to the best-selling *Born to Run: A Hidden Tribe, Superathletes, and the Greatest Race the World Has Never Seen*. In it, he concluded that the best shoe might, in fact, be none at all—and in the process revealed much about what makes our species special.

A pivotal clue lay in McDougall's crossing paths with the work of an eccentric South African, who in turn sought to understand the archaic hunting methods of a little-known tribe.

The riddle biologist Louis Liebenberg sought to solve had long confounded evolutionists. Fossil evidence suggested Homo sapiens's ancestors had descended from the trees to the savanna 200,000 years ago in search of meat to feed their growing brains. Yet archaeological evidence showed humans only started to bring down larger, faster prey with stone-tipped weapons in 120,000 years later. Thus, a confounding question: How did we get meat all that time?

In the 1980s, Liebenberg discovered that Namibia's Ju/'hoansi San people still hunted without stone tips. The key to their technique was where his interests intersected with McDougall's: running. What Liebenberg called "persistence hunting" entailed tracking prey over vast distances for days until the animal was so exhausted it could be surrounded and killed with simple wood spears.

Kinesthesiologists confirmed that the human body, from our fur-free bodies to our articulated legs, appeared to have evolved to outrun almost any large animal.

This only scratched the surface of Liebenberg's research, whose depths were hinted at by the curious title of his 1990 study,

The Art of Tracking: The Origin of Science. Humans' evolved ability to run weekly ultramarathons was necessary but not sufficient. What about all the other capabilities required to hunt? The ability to spot and make sense of clues indicating the path of prey? To empathize with the plight of a wounded, cornered animal, imagining where it might go next?

And these were just the *individual* skills required. Persistence hunting could only work as a group activity. How did we learn to coordinate? To divvy up and master specialized roles, from bush-beating to water-bearing? Adapt to changes caused by the warming climate, like shrinking water supplies and reduced foliage cover? Develop and pass on new and better techniques?

The acquisition of such abilities helped us grow, over millennia, into a species that could learn, well, whatever we needed to learn. It helped us cross deserts, mountains, and oceans; live in ever larger and more complex communities; and thrive in almost any environment, from rainforests to the tundra.

We became, as Liebenberg put it, "natural scientists."

What's remarkable about this for present purposes is the particular style of collaboration that allowed Homo sapiens to compensate for and even leverage our individual vulnerabilities and differences.

Collaboration itself was not distinctive. Other hominids, like Neanderthals and Homo erectus, worked in groups. So did primates like chimps and gorillas.

But something was different about human groups. They involved individual specialization, adaptation, and strategy. They were less gangs or swarms than teams.

The core question evolutionary biologists seek to answer is this: Why do humans have psychological tendencies that seem maladaptive in post-evolutionary life, like depression and anxiety? The premise on which they look to construct a solution is the observation that evolution could not have been a rational act. Primitive humans did not have families with a view to passing on gene sequences. Likewise, what led us to form enduring groups were not calculations so much as emotional inclinations that survive to this day. The field's leading figures, from founder Edward O. Wilson to psychologist Mark van Vugt and others, frequently point to a factor one rarely hears about from scientists: the necessity of "a shared purpose or identity in social formation."

In his ground-breaking 1975 *Sociobiology: A New Synthesis*, Wilson observes:

> *The most important property of a group is its purpose. Without a purpose, a group is nothing more than a collection of individuals.... Our ability to cooperate is our key survival advantage.*

What allowed us to survive when our rivals didn't was not just a matter of skill, but will. To live in ever larger and more complex tribes (other animals' packs get to a certain size and stay there), individual humans had to be not only able but keen to embrace specialized roles we had not been born into instinctively, like, say, bees.

Where we parted ways with other hominids was our love of change and adaptation. Erectus spread to South East Asia but disappeared when warming temperatures thinned out tree cover required to hunt, and they proved unable to modify their methods. Whereas Sapiens loved taking on roles that were different, not just from their ancestors' but that they themselves might have played earlier in their own lives.

All this sounds reasonable, and, in light of what we've discussed in chapters 1 and 3, familiar.

Could this be why we needed a feeling of purpose? To keep us dedicated to supporting the changing needs of our groups?

If so, how did we lose it?

WHERE THINGS WENT WRONG

If we have a natural propensity for purpose, per Wilson *et al.*—and to talk about things that aren't working (chapter 1)—the fact that we are now talking about WHY more than ever (chapters 2 and 3) positions our present purpose crisis as a distinctly modern phenomenon.

How have things gone off the rails? How has this natural inclination become so rarely satisfied, a source of confusion and even pain?

Six developments, presented here in roughly chronological order, have played a part. Understanding them is critical to crafting a solution.

1. Civilization

Population growth put distance between individual efforts and collective needs. It's one thing to feel impact on a tribe of one or two hundred. But a hundred thousand, or million? Not so straightforward.

It isn't just that individuals felt less personally important as communities grew in size and scope. It also became less clear what kind of impact we should even be trying to have—what a "good" person should do to make a difference.

For most of his mid-twentieth century career, the economist Friedrich Hayek remained zealously preoccupied with what he felt to be the greatest danger facing humanity: the rise of central planning, or government-driven resource allocation. For most of our history, Hayek argued, human beings had lived in relatively small communities where the calculus of how individual behavior might impact the group was all but self-evident. This was, in turn, reflected in our cultural values: the actions members of a given community generally believed to be right or wrong.

In groups with several dozen or a few hundred members, one could have enough information to understand how one's individual behavior impacted the group—when it might make sense to sacrifice one's own interest for that of the whole. Our cultural values reflected this: putting the group first was good, self-interest bad.

In larger communities, however, the dynamic changed. No one individual or group could ever have enough information to know which needs should be prioritized. That role fell to decentralized expressions of needs and solutions, aka markets, which generated prices that could indicate what the society needs more and less of.

The challenge? Our sense of what we can do to have impact was based on cultural traditions from simpler times. Humans did not intuitively understand the economic systems that made modern life so much more abundant and complicated than primitive communities. Most of us, thus, instinctively feel that centralized solutions to problems like poverty pollution should work, even if they are not up to the task, as the most centralized systems of all (communist countries) tragically demonstrated. In Hayek's view, humanity's challenge was to replace cultural nostalgia with a better understanding of how the modern world's "extended order" worked.

As we saw in chapter 3, similar cultural habit runs deep in our modern intuitions about purpose. This may explain why so much of our language is vague, even mystical ("I feel *called* to impact *something bigger than myself*"). Yet, we're surprised to discover these intuitions don't always lead to clarity, or even intended results.

Is working for a social enterprise or cleantech company really the best way to help the world? We've met many working for such organizations who have developed strong doubts (see chapter 7).

Might we do as much or more by investing more effort into helping our companies deliver more customer joy? Milton Friedman and Chris Rock (chapter 1) would appear to think so.

Bottom line: The path to positive social impact has become far from obvious, even as the drive to have it remains.

2. Specialization

The Industrial Revolution was more than a technological shift.

Starting in the 1760s, new methods for producing iron and steel enabled mass production of machines, in turn growing other production. Steam helped machines increase output, along with locomotives and ships that broadened distribution. Electric power multiplied all this. The telegraph facilitated communication and grew markets.

None of this happened without changes in human behavior. It became increasingly rare for individuals to turn raw materials into finished product. Process managers stationed them at fixed positions so they could become more efficient and waste less time moving around.

The most eye-opening attempt to understand this transformation came from Adam Smith. The first chapter of his *Wealth of Nations* laid out the core principle of modern economics in its title:

"Of the Division of Labour."

A lone pin maker, Smith observed, might be able to make twenty pins a day. Working as part of a ten-person factory line, say, putting the heads on, she might effectively produce hundreds.

Smith was far from alone in seeing this functional specialization as the key to productivity growth. It developed expertise, reduced errors, and saved time. At the dawn of the twentieth century, carmaker Henry Ford showed how assembly lines could mass produce complex goods with thousands of parts. A hundred years later, Amazon used similar principles to lower costs so much that it was able to capture nearly half of all consumer e-commerce.

Yet the wealth creation miracle all this drove—a sixteenfold increase in individual output from 1800 to the present—have come with a devastating psychological toll. Specialized workers may be far more productive than their predecessors. But few can point to a single product they've made themselves. Unless they're in sales or customer service (representing less than a fifth of American jobs as of 2022), most are unlikely to ever meet a customer. They cannot, in short, feel their true impact.

The implications of this were not immediately obvious as specialization exploded, but soon became unmissable. Nineteenth century employees began to experience unprecedented levels of disorientation, dissatisfaction, and purposelessness. A sense of being "mentally debased," as the economist Karl Marx put it, led millions to embrace his political prescriptions like a religion, with tragic consequences: the twentieth century's communist regimes, from Stalin's Russia to Mao's China, killed tens of millions.

To make things worse, the benefits began to shrink (chapter 1). Productivity gains from specialization leveled off in the 1950s and '60s before falling into secular decline. The gulf between work and impact widened. A 2019 survey found that 89 percent of US companies ranked "customer experience" among their top success drivers, while less than a third of jobs were customer-facing. Millions were left feeling deficient in either pay or purpose—and often both. As HubSpot CEO Yamini Rangan put it, the modern workplace faced "a crisis of disconnection."

3. Choice

In 1959, a future president of Bell Labs took a break from researching lasers to write about a curious phenomenon he'd begun to observe outside of work.

Economic theory held choice to be a good thing, the more the better. William Baker suspected otherwise. When an individual was presented with options without enough information or time to evaluate them—like deciding what car to buy when you need one for your new job the next day—a "paradox of choice" arose. Fear of choosing wrong and living to regret a purchase could outweigh the value of the product.

This concept gained increasing interest among late twentieth-century economists and sociologists, including "bounded rationality" theorist Herbert Simon, before being popularized by psychologist Barry Schwartz and sociologist Renata Salecl. "Today we are encouraged to view our lives as being full of choice," Salecl wrote in 2011's *The Tyranny of Choice:*

> *Like products on a supermarket shelf, our identities seem to be there for the choosing. But paradoxically, this freedom can create anxiety, and feelings of guilt and inadequacy... late capitalism's shrill exhortations to "be yourself" are leading to ever-greater disquiet.*

Such anxiety arose not simply from purchasing decisions, but any kind of life choice, including where to live, where to go to school—and what career to pursue.

4. Comparison

Because human beings have few instincts compared to other animals, we learn how to behave primarily through imitation. The little brother accused of "being a copycat" by his annoyed sister is only doing what our ancestors have done since the beginning of time.

Adults likewise tend to make and evaluate their decisions by looking at those they consider successful and/or happy. Studies show we're generally less concerned with how well we're doing in absolute terms than relative to those around us: As social psychologist Susan Fiske puts it, "We are comparison machines,".

In the modern world, this natural practice has become far more complicated because our comparison set has exploded. With the rise of mass media, we now compare and contrast ourselves with celebrities we'll likely never meet. The psychological impact has been overwhelming, shrinking the perceived value of our everyday accomplishments and elevating that of wildly imaginative "dreams."

Consider: Until the mid-twentieth century, an entrepreneur who built a company employing hundreds of people was likely to feel like a success. With the advent of modern venture capital and technological scalability, however, the bar has been raised. If you aren't running a Silicon Valley unicorn or large public company, you're just another small-time CEO. (When raising capital for our own start-ups, we often heard, "Great idea, but can it scale to a billion dollars?")

When it comes to purpose, the rise of celebrity self-help and life-coaching has produced, paradoxically, similar discouragement. Many are attracted by the success of an Oprah or Tony Robbins, who tell them they can have it if they want it enough. Yet such figures, who position themselves as "life coaches," are in many ways poor guides. Typically they have come to enjoy their own success not merely from factors they're aware of, but a fortunate, hard-to-replicate set of circumstances they are hard put to explain. What's left? Frequently questionable exhortations such as:

Success is doing what you want, when you want, where you want, with whom you want, as much as you want.

Really? As our sights are raised to such levels, so is our capacity for despair. Rates of teen depression, self-harm, and suicide have all but paralleled the rise of social media and "influencers."

Adults are not far behind.

5. *Toxicity*

Once upon a time, a "toxic work environment" was one in which ambient chemicals might impact the health of employees, especially expectant mothers.

In the mid '90s, political scientist Marcia Lynn Whicker appropriated the term to describe another danger: management styles that undermine performance and well-being. Once the thing had a name, millions took interest, revealing its widespread nature (see Exhibit 6.2).

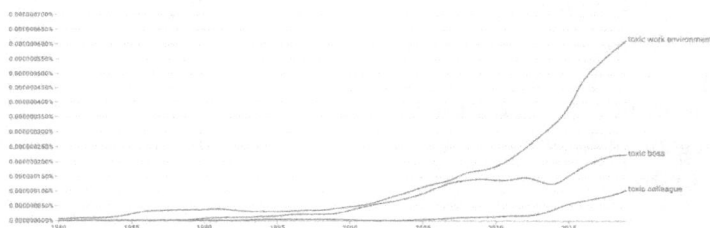

Exhibit 6.2: *The rise of interest in workplace toxicity, 1980–2019*
Source: Google Ngram Viewer

A recent MIT study lists the symptoms of workplace toxicity: disrespect (especially to juniors), bullying, abuse, cliquishness, and unethical practice. Managers, of course, are not the only source of such behavior—pity the new head of a securities trading desk who must deal with the industry's seemingly interminable "bro" culture. But in most toxic work environments, they are at least enablers. The costs astonish: Among the 40 percent of US employees who've considered changing jobs in recent years, toxicity matters more than ten times as much as compensation.

One HR expert we work with articulates the common thread of such behavior as "focusing on goals other than those of the company." This is helpful, but it also kicks the can down the road. What causes leaders to fall out of alignment?

The answer lies in a combination of skill shortcomings (inexperience, lack of role models, poor judgment, weak communication), psychological challenges (immaturity, emotional insecurity, career misery), and hierarchical cultures (authoritarianism, upwardly focused politics). The last factor may be the biggest culprit, for only a hierarchical culture would put people with skill shortcomings and psychological challenges in positions of authority—who then mistake stress for inspiration, overwork for productivity, and sexism for spirit, all sadly familiar in Silicon Valley.

In the absence of strong systems for tracking managerial effectiveness—specifically those related to employee development and engagement, as we'll see in chapter 8—managers' managers naturally tend to focus on what's directly in front of them: personal relationships and their reports' self-presentation. Such lack of objectivity drives cynicism through the ranks, even when leaders at the top are well-meaning and viewed favorably. It also contributes to other engagement-killing ills, including inequitable pay and a lack of diversity in senior ranks.

6. Metrics

This leads us to our last workplace purpose killer.

In a 1977 article, "The Story of Joe (A Fable)," BCG founder Bruce Henderson tracked the journey of a well-intentioned but hapless manager. Joe became a company star by turning money-losing divisions into profitable ones, yet still ended up being fired. Why? Because his MO was to slash costs, sell assets, and kill investment projects without regard for long-term consequences. The result was short-term upticks that soured, leaving disaster in their wake. Henderson noted that the company was as much to blame as Joe, who was only optimizing what was, on paper, valued. The moral: Even well-meaning managers can do harm if assessed by the wrong metrics.

Such situations commonly arise as organizations scale and develop subcultures. By the time a firm joins the Fortune 500, some divisions may well be flourishing under the legacy of a good boss (and those they've mentored and elevated), while others find themselves struggling under a legacy of bad ones (who have brought along other toxic managers like themselves). While firms often invest in corporate tools to expose such variations, including divisional engagement surveys, retention, churn statistics, and Diversity, Equity, Inclusion, and Belonging [DEIB] metrics), they often fail to take the results seriously or act on the team-by-team data they produce. Frontline employees in worse-performing areas doubt their employers are actually committed to their strategic and values lines. The tragic cycle continues.

The good news? Enterprise leaders have a series of powerful tools in their corner, many of which, as we'll see in chapter 8, revolve around purpose.

INTERNALIZING THE RIGHT PURPOSE

In 1962, marine biologist Rachel Carson published a 368-page attack on the growing industrial use of toxic pesticides. *Silent Spring* became an overnight success: the first bestseller of the nascent environmental movement, and still, to many, its bible.

Eight years later, *Silent Spring* inspired a young couple in Kennebunkport, Maine—a recently graduated English major and a sculptor—to found a company producing natural personal-care products. In time, Tom's of Maine would not only become a leading brand but a highly rewarding venture for Tom and Kate Chappell. Their initial $5,000 investment would yield years of healthy dividends and, in 2006, a $100 million exit.

Few employees in the late-twentieth-century personal-care industry came to work with the energizing purpose of those at Tom's of Maine. Ironically, Tom himself wasn't one of them. While he genuinely cared about the harmful chemicals in most personal-care products, his primary driver had been the market opportunity suggested by Carson's success. By the mid-80s, he'd become listless, taking a leave of absence to pursue a divinity degree. When he returned, he instituted changes, including a new policy that allowed employees to donate up to 5 percent of their time to local causes.

What happened next is not well documented. By one account, however, the reaction was the opposite of what the Chappells intended. Some employees were enthused by the idea. Others weren't. If some of their time was better spent working for a charity rather than the company mission, why not all of it?

This story highlights two important insights when it comes to feeling purposeful at work that will inform the next two chapters.

First, as Tom Chappell discovered for himself, perceptions of purpose are personal. Founding and running a transformative company won't make you feel purposeful if it's not the impact you most care about.* The second draws on a theme we articulated in chapter 2 and shall explore further in chapter 9. Extrinsic rewards not related directly to our daily work are not as motivating as intrinsic ones (in a sense, the volunteering option at Tom's of Maine was just another benefit or form of compensation). A talented product designer generally feels better about developing a feature that makes a product more successful than doing pro bono work or hearing that her firm has made a big donation. Furthermore, many employees share the sentiment expressed by Brazilian industrialist Ricardo Semler: "if you're giving back, you've taken too much."

Companies and purpose consultants alike often fail to appreciate the importance of the extrinsic/intrinsic distinction. They talk about corporate citizenship initiatives to impress millennials and Gen Zers, both as their consumers and employees. This is important, even necessary, for employees, as surveys tell us. But hearing about these initiatives does not provide the kind of built-in purpose that fires them up to do their best work and become more productive.

Many may draw some sense of pride from being part of a company that supports worthy causes, particularly when they have some say in what the causes are. As we've seen from figures like Friedman and Beinhocker, however, there is a powerful argument to be made that companies—and by extension, their people—do far more good by producing better products at lower prices that appeal to larger numbers, thus creating consumer, producer, and even stakeholder surplus.

Would employees not feel even more engaged and energized in their work if they understood this mysterious and arguably counter-

---

* Chappell ultimately found a personal fit, as detailed in his memoir *The Soul of a Business*, but it was not a straight line.

intuitive dynamic, as Hayek wished for his readers? What if the emotional reward for doing their work was the work itself? What if their WHY and the company's WHY were clearly aligned? ⌀⇁

KEY TAKEAWAYS   ֎

1. Psychologists agree on three components of happiness/well-
    being: physical health, gratitude, and giving.

2. Our need for purpose is closely related to our propensity to give.
    To understand that need, we must delve into where it comes from
    and how it works in our psychology.

3. Evolutionary biology posits that our emotional reward system is
    largely unchanged from that which helped us survive and thrive
    tens of millennia ago.

4. Homo sapiens had a distinct survival advantage from other homi-
    nids: a proclivity for working adaptively in groups, inspired by
    the satisfaction we get from having a specific, adaptive impact
    on others.

5. Sociobiologists believe this need to feel purpose inspired us to
    take on specialized roles in collaborative team-like structures,
    compensating for individual physical vulnerability.

6. The knowledge we acquired and passed on allowed humans to
    start adapting our environment to ourselves, moving the venue
    of evolutionary progress (trial, error, success, and reproduction)
    from our genes to our societies and cultures.

7. We lost our original, clear, purpose feeling through several devel-
    opments:

    a. *Civilization* and the growing scale of society, which put distance
        between individual efforts and collective needs, complicating
        our intuitions regarding what we "should" be doing.

    b. *Specialization* in jobs following the Industrial Revolution, when it
        became clear that this model was the basis of modern produc-
        tivity but further disconnected us from our impact on others.

    c. *Choice* which ballooned as a by-product of economic growth
        and raised our levels of anxiety and regret, including in
        our careers.

    d. *Comparisons* we began making between ourselves and famous
        individuals and companies with the rise of mass media,
        fostering unrealistic expectations.

    e. *Toxicity* awareness in the workplace, as social media made it easier to share stories of managers with personal agendas.

    f. *Metrics* used to assess managers that were primarily financial and glossed over employee engagement.

8. Purpose must be embraced as an individual, internalized feeling that we can access directly at and through our work—one of the most powerful motivators we have.

9. Companies must walk their talk if they are to inspire consumer and employee trust, and promote that purpose-feeling.

PART THREE: *TOWARD A NEW WHY*

SCARECROW

What about the heart that you promised Tin Man?

WIZARD

Well, I...

SCARECROW

And the courage that you promised Cowardly Lion?

WIZARD

Well, I...

TIN MAN AND LION

And Scarecrow's brain?

WIZARD

Well, I—but you've got them. You've had them all the time!

NOEL LANGLEY, FLORENCE RYERSON, AND
EDGAR ALLEN WOOLF
THE WIZARD OF OZ (1939)

CHAPTER 7

What Employees Must Do

"Do the best you can in every task, no matter how unimportant it may seem at the time. No one learns more about a problem than the person at the bottom."

SANDRA DAY O'CONNOR

B ARELY TWO YEARS INTO HER CAREER, "Anika" was feeling stuck.

She *thought* she had her dream job. Growing up in a family that prized education, she'd gone to college hoping to become a teacher in marginalized communities. A challenging practicum experience, however, led her to reassess her talents. She'd switched her major to business, hoping instead to land a place with a socially minded edtech company.

In "ChalkCo," a digital math learning platform that subsidized free elementary courses out of paid secondary ones, Anika believed she'd found the perfect match. As a business analyst, her role was to understand the net value of the company's offerings. Her teammates shared her passion for social impact. Her boss cared about her progress. What else could a purpose-driven twentysomething ask for?

By the time we met Anika as part of a strategy engagement, her enthusiasm was flagging. Her early work had led to meaningful change, notably the launch of a free high school math offering. Since then, however, the data had grown more complex, the ahas rarer, the action items more ambiguous. Worse, competitive pressures had started weighing on ChalkCo. As concerns about cash began to eclipse social entrepreneurship, she found it harder to figure out what difference her work was making, if any.

Anika was the one who told us, "I often feel like a musician who can't hear themselves play."
The more we thought about that statement, the more we were struck by its implications. It figured in our recommendations to ChalkCo and helped us develop a program to address the WHY challenge that inspired this project (chapter 1).

Why have we come to see this analogy as so important? It focused us on two things:

1. *Our need for purpose is, at its heart, a need to feel our impact on others and our world.*

If we can't sense our impact—typically because our place in an organization leaves us with limited perspective on or connection to the customer who benefits from our work, internal or external—we are likely to feel purpose-deficient.

2. *Just as an electric guitarist or keyboardist must plug their instrument into an amp to hear themselves play, workers must plug into meaningful individual feedback loops in order to feel their impact.*

This is easier said than done. But it can be done—if both employees and managers appreciate what's required of them.

Chapter 8 will dig into what this means for companies. Leaders must align their talk with their walk by using appropriate metrics—in effect, "amps" for managers—to hold leaders at all levels accountable for their impact on employees. In turn, managers must provide their teams with timely feedback loops so they can sense their impact. When employees can internalize their purpose by "hearing" their impact, feeling the impact of their daily work within the louder "music" of the company, they do better and get better and feel better. They are able to play their essential role in value creation, combining knowledge and empathy to produce innovation (chapters 4 and 5).

But they need to come to the table ready to listen and grow, with a strong understanding of their own role and aims. This chapter explores what we have found an individual purpose practice must incorporate, including:

1. The *principles* of how individual purpose works,
2. A working *paradigm* of the factors individuals can influence to produce that purpose, and
3. Emerging best *practices* for making this work.

PRINCIPLES OF INDIVIDUAL PURPOSE

A paradigm is a way of stripping down a complex thing into its key parts. Thus simplified, we can more effectively understand and interact with it. Often, but not necessarily, this process involves mapping courses of action and predicting outcomes through a visualization.

We've already touched on several paradigms throughout this book, like microeconomics' supply and demand curves, Jim Collins's Hedgehog (a corporate purpose paradigm), and Simon Sinek's Golden Circle (a personal WHY paradigm).

To understand their part in organizational purpose, individuals need an accessible yet psychologically sound personal paradigm that incorporates these principles:*

1. To experience well-being, humans need to feel as though they are having meaningful impact on others: purpose.
2. To feel meaningful impact on others, we must sense a fit between ourselves (our energies, passions, and capabilities) and the needs of others that we can address: what we call "Self-Impact Fit." This is not itself a feeling of purpose, but the essential precondition for experiencing it. Self-Impact Fit is the stage we need to find

---

* By "principles" we mean, per Ray Dalio, founder of the world's largest hedge fund, "fundamental truths that serve as the foundations for behavior that gets you what you want out of life. They can be applied again and again in similar situations to help you achieve your goals."

our way onto; WHY is the performance.

3. All three aspects of this fit change over time, to greater or lesser extents, because the world changes over time.

4. Thus, it's unlikely that most will discover Self-Impact Fit through a "one and done" reflection. Self-Impact Fit and WHY are moving targets that we can only discover through action and may land on for longer or shorter periods. Most lives and careers are journeys through a series of meaningful WHYs.

When we recognized the need for this personal paradigm, our hope was to find one that was singular and elegant. As economists, physicists, and others have discovered, however, a single paradigm is not always practical or useful. Dynamics often change with changes in scale or perspective, much as economics comes in micro and macro flavors and physics lacks a Grand Unified Theory.

We found the workings of individual purpose to be best understood at two levels:

*   A *WHERE* paradigm to identify where we should search for Self-Impact Fit (The Self-Impact Compass), and
*   A *HOW* paradigm for recognizing when we are experiencing WHY (*The WHY Iceberg*).

THE WHERE PARADIGM: THE SELF-IMPACT COMPASS

Companies exist to solve human problems (chapter 4). As people who work for companies, finding our individual purpose and maximizing our impact is a question of finding where and how we can contribute to solutions and best serve others' needs. This has as much to do with the problems others believe we can solve as our ability and passion to solve them. All three elements are the compo-nents of Self-Impact Fit, wherein we can find our WHY. We won't do ourselves any favors by assuming that Self-Impact Fit or WHY is easy to find. Neither can be discovered without sustained work.

Harvard Business School's Jon M. Jachimowicz makes a similar observation about the related concept of work "passion":

> *One common misperception people have about passion is that it is fixed: You either have passion for something or you don't. The problem with this belief is that it's limiting, leading us to think of passion as something we discover or happen upon, and we may not take into account the fact that it often takes time to develop one's passion for a job, along with the skills, confidence, and rela-tionships that allow one to experience passion for work.*

Given the importance of definitions in this complex area (chapter 3), let's start by defining what we're talking about.

"Self" is something we all experience but whose nature has long been debated. For present purposes, we can define it as a singu-lar cluster of inclinations, associations, memories, and capabilities, which distinguishes us from others and which we identify and expe-rience more or less continuously. (Sleep is an interruption, but we generally remember who we are when we wake up.)

In practical terms, our sense of self reconciles two distinct and potentially opposed psychological requirements:

- *Our need for sensory stability* (to help distinguish between our physical persons and the world around us, helping us operate), and
- *Our need for variety*, which makes the search for the things we need and can improve our lots.

The persistent patterns of behavior associated with our selves form our personalities. These become relatively stable in adulthood, to the point of often seeming unchanging, though they're not. Psycholo-gists point out that our personalities change with age and experience:

we tend to become less social and more agreeable, for example.

The evolution of our personality over time has significant implications for our experience of WHY. Purpose is a feeling of impact on the world. If we suppose the only impact worth discovering is a *life* purpose, we are effectively (if unconsciously) assuming that neither we nor the world are going to change very much, which is a pretty big assumption.

It may be possible to define a lifelong purpose if we pitch it at such a generalized level that it's unlikely to change ("I fix things," "I help people feel better"). For some professions—in this example, mechanics and health-care professionals, respectively—these may prove meaningful. Google "individual WHY statement examples," however, and you'll see just how vague most lifelong WHY statements tend to be. This vagueness ensures that they have limited value as guides to action. "I help others lead happier lives," for example, could apply to virtually anyone in any job and is unlikely to shape a WHY feeling, which relates to our special contribution. Yet specific WHY statements ("I develop user-friendly mobile apps," "I sell environmentally friendly products") tend to have shorter shelf lives than we do. That's not a bad thing, as both our selves and the parts of the world we wish to impact change over time, but we need to be upfront with ourselves about that and not cling to such a statement beyond its sell-by date.

It's not impossible to find a form of impact that evolves in tandem with the changing world and our changing selves over the course of a forty-year career, like the mechanic and health care examples. But this is not the norm. The average employee changes jobs almost ten times before they turn forty. For most, finding Self-Impact Fit is an evergreen, lifelong endeavor. This is not to say it takes a lifetime to find, just that it is something we must find and refind, over and over, as our growth and/or circumstances require.

If we shrink the area in which to find our WHY, and lessen the pressure to find one that lasts forever, the process becomes simple and the results more meaningful. To demonstrate this, let's turn to our paradigms, starting with the Self-Impact Compass.

Exhibit 7.1: The Self-Impact Compass
Source: Stephen Butler and Karissa Price

The Compass has three main parts: our passions or energies, our know-how, and others' needs. Here's what we mean by each:

1. *Our Passions or Energies.* We cannot have much impact doing something we don't like to do or, more precisely, get no energy from doing. We may be able to make a go of it for a while, say, if the money is good or we're driven by some other necessity, like following a life partner. But over time, it is all but impossible to sustain a good fit with something that drains us, whether that's work we find highly repetitive (in a bad way) or an activity we enjoyed in the past but now makes us feel burned out.

2. *Our Know-How.* It's not enough to want to be able to have a particular kind of impact, like being a sought-after medical specialist, a jet-setting crypto trader, or a professional athlete. We have to be good at it. What we call know-how encompasses two aspects that we'll unpack in the next section: 1) what we can already do (our capabilities) and 2) what positions us to innovate, i.e., our ability to generate insight.

3. *Others' Needs.* The first two factors speak to who we are and our ability to solve problems. This third part defines the problems we might solve. This is trickier than the others, for the simple reason that it's not entirely up to us to determine what needs we can serve. We cannot do whatever job we believe we're qualified for, no matter how much we think we can. Those whose needs we wish to serve (customers) or those with whom we wish to work to deliver service (employers) need to find us and decide that we're capable.

Situations and Strategies

Why call this a compass? Because it does more than help us understand what drives Self-Impact Fit. It helps diagnose where we feel deficient and, thus, get a sense of where we need to go.

The first step in using the Self-Impact Compass is to locate ourselves. Think about your current situation and aspirations. Assess how you feel about your work along each of these three dimensions (tools are suggested later in this chapter): How much do you love the work? How qualified do you feel to do it well? How qualified does your current or potential employer believe you are?

This places you in one of eight possible situations, including not feeling satisfied with anything (the different sets depicted in Exhibit 7.1). For purposes of brevity, we will jump over the latter and the four where we are only feeling satisfied on one dimension (e.g., feeling passionate about something but have no skills or opportunities to pursue it). Once we've grasped the tactics for negotiating the others, the implications should be evident.

The situations in which we feel satisfied with two out of three components are these:

- *Situation 1: Dream.* This is when we are doing work we love and are good at but are not currently getting paid to do. Many great works, businesses, and careers have started this way, as a kind of hobby. But this cannot be a locus of Self-Impact Fit until someone is willing to pay us.

Strategy: Find your market, i.e., someone who will pay you. This might involve better self-marketing, moving to a place where such jobs are more common, and/or choosing something else that you love doing or are good at with better prospects.

- *Situation 2: Impostor.* Impostor syndrome occurs when we find ourselves paid to do work where we don't feel we have the skills to do it well. This feeling is more common than most realize; studies suggest it impacts up to four in five early in their careers. While the experience is often subjective—particularly among women who experience high societal standards and hold themselves to even higher personal ones—many slip into roles that exceed our capabilities (particularly in frontline management, as we'll see in chapter 8). The key here is to see this situation not as someone else's mistake, but to appreciate that luck plays a role in success, and to view yours as an opportunity to achieve Self-Impact Fit.

    Strategy: Develop your know-how through experience, mentorship, formal and informal training, or some combination thereof.

- *Situation 3: Drudge.* When we are capable and valued but care little about the impact we're having, we get bored. Drudgery feeing is common in two situations: early in our working lives, when we realize the career we've chosen is less exciting than we expected (a common experience among young lawyers), and later, when we've done the same thing so long that we burn out.

    Strategy: Change goals. Pivot to other roles or sectors where your skills may be used or set new challenges within your current role/sector (like a CEO raising their firm's growth targets).

Structural Challenges

Align all three areas of the Compass and you've achieved Self-Impact Fit: a place where you can experience the sense of WHY we hunger after. Is it really that simple? Is it time to move on to understanding what this feels like?

Not yet. It's first necessary to note that not all dimensions are equally subject to our influence.

Start with Needs. Life coaches often encourage us to see our dreams as something we can will into reality; we "just" need to find our market, meet the right people, and, with enough hustle, we'll be successful. * This overlooks the role luck plays. Yes, a healthy person with the right education and financial resources might make their own luck, or at least improve their odds by, say, networking. For most of us, our prospects are limited by the absence of such advantages and other factors beyond our control, from where and when we were born, to personal and family obligations, and so on.

Nor do we really have much say over our Passions. "Don't do what you love, love what you do" has become a career advice chestnut. Those who repeat it, however, have clearly never had much exposure to drudgery. No matter how hard we try, we can't simply make ourselves be energized by something we vehemently dislike.

The third part of the Self-Impact Compass, however—"Know-How"—that we can do something about. So much so that it forms that basis of our HOW paradigm.

THE HOW PARADIGM: THE WHY ICEBERG

WHY may look like it's simply about impact. But impact doesn't just happen in isolation. Many processes make it possible, and they are all part of living our WHY.

By the time Anika started to question her place at ChalkCo, a member of the company's mobile team, "Vlad," was already losing sleep over a more existential concern: keeping his job.

Mobile had never been core to ChalkCo's PC-based business. Vlad's team had been formed as an experiment: to see if an AI-powered app could function as a virtual tutor. The results had been baffling. The product helped learners improve skills dramatically. Schools downloaded the app in huge numbers. Then... they barely used it.

The team was at a loss. The product should have been a home

---

* Indeed, this premise has allowed their industry to expand rapidly in recent years; otherwise, their target market would be smaller and practitioner skill requirements greater.

run. Knowing their jobs were at stake, they put in long hours trying to figure out the problem.

As a tester, Vlad was not expected to help. His role was to ensure each release worked as intended. But he was also the father of a nine-year-old whose school was trialing ChalkCo's app. One day, Vlad asked his daughter's teacher what she thought. "It works," she said, "but I don't know how. So I can't recommend it to parents."

It wasn't hard to see how the insight had slipped between the cracks. The user experience group focused on kids' usage. Sales talked to teachers, but they were more concerned with adding schools than parents. All missed the fact that elementary teachers, who knew little about AI or were often weak in math themselves, were embarrassed that they had trouble understanding how this technology worked.

At the next morning's stand up, Vlad shared the teacher's comment, nervous that he was stepping out of his role. Everyone listened politely before the product manager stepped forward—and applauded. The team had been so impressed with the product's effectiveness they missed how intimidating it was to a key part of the market. They quickly got to work on a training video campaign that helped teachers get it, turned the mobile flop into a hit, and saved their jobs.

Vlad's story illustrates an important truth about how we can find purpose in virtually any job. The search itself—how we seek information to generate new insight—is part and parcel of our WHY.

Here's the thinking.

If feeling impact is about solving problems, our search for that feeling must include the full process of how we solve problems, and how this factors into what WHY feels like.

To solve problems, we need know-how, i.e., relevant knowledge and skills. Putting our company's general know-how to use (in this case, the app), however, requires specific insight into the situation where it's used. Whether we're a mechanic repairing an engine or a marketer figuring out why a product isn't selling, existing knowledge is not enough; we need to know which part has worn out or which aspect of the purchasing experience is turning customers off. To innovate successfully and beat competitors, we must, per Alain de Botton, discover an aspect of reality others haven't seen.

Living purpose at work is not just about actually having impact but doing the discovery work required to enable insight. Obvious moments of impact—fixing a car, landing a new client, developing a new product feature—are the easiest to recognize and celebrate. But such moments don't happen in isolation. They can't happen without all the work it takes to build enough know-how to recognize a problem, empathize with clients, understand their needs, then deliver an impactful solution.

Insights may come to us without looking, like the proverbial apple dropping on Isaac Newton's head. But they happen more often when we're leaning into our natural curiosity. This doesn't mean we all need to see ourselves as scientists, getting into the nitty-gritty of how things work, thinking about the forces of the universe. As we learned from Louis Liebenberg in chapter 6, we are already natural scientists. All the time we're discovering TV shows and music, we can be figuring out faster ways to reach our destinations, working out the best way to live within our means. All that is discovery and knowledge creation. The value of this is exemplified in the rise of social media influencing—a $20 billion (and growing) industry built on the insights of thousands of mini experts.

So in which of our daily activities are we living our purpose—developing knowledge or using it?

Both.

Impact is simply the tip of what we call The WHY Iceberg (Exhibit 7.2). Like any iceberg tip, it cannot exist without the rest of the iceberg—in this case, perpetual discovery and know-how creation. Impact can't exist without these any more than a championship team can exist without practice or a Nobel Prize without research.

What leads us to overlook or discount these other activities in our minds is that they happen at different speeds. Notable moments of impact are relatively rare. Flashes of insight that set us up for such moments are more frequent. The seeking that leads to insight happens nearly all the time, without noticing. The key to increasing our purpose-feeling is to notice: to be mindful of the whole Iceberg.

Exhibit 7.2: The WHY Iceberg
Source: Stephen Butler and Karissa Price

This holistic view of WHY points to how we can feel purposeful in almost any job.

Vlad's story shows the Iceberg in action. The *impact* he had was evident: He saved a twenty-person team and a great product from the scrap heap. He achieved that impact by forming *know-how*, the insight into teachers' ignorance and embarrassment. That, in turn, came from his own curiosity that led him to approach his child's teacher: *discovery*.

Framed this way, it's relatively easy to appreciate how Vlad was living his WHY all along. What's essential for us is to see how this story is not unusual but typical. Those with outstanding achievements often remark that their whole lives seem to have let to that moment. In fact, anytime we impact anything, we can retrospectively see how many things, intentional or not, contributed to it, from our education to our experience to being in the right place at the right time.

Retrospective appreciation is easy. The key to recognizing ourselves as living in and fulfilling our WHY in the present, indeed, all the time, is to recognize how our activities may lead to such moments. We may have no way of knowing which activities will make the difference. Our theory of our WHY helps us focus our activities and increase the odds of impact.

Vlad's curiosity, his risk to voice what he uncovered, paid off. But what if it hadn't? What if another colleague had identified the blind spot first—or if there turned out to be no way to address the teachers' concerns? Would Vlad's efforts have been for nothing? Would he have had no purpose?

Not at all. His perpetual discovery will lead to other impact. In fact, that's what he does every day by trying to find flaws in new products. And when he doesn't, there's always another kind of impact he's having: on *himself.* Any time we learn or generate an insight that stays with us, whether we ultimately use it or not, we are increasing our own potential to have future impact.

Now, how do we turn these insights into action?

PROMISING PRACTICES

Much of the life coaching industry is built on programs that prescribe progressive step programs. One of the most comprehensive is Mastin Kipp's *Claim Your Power,* which maps a forty-day journey toward thriving in "your life's unique purpose."

The appeal of such programs is evident, akin to a diet or workout regimen. Breaking a complex act of transformation into discrete parts makes it more approachable and practicable.

It is tempting to read too much into their sequencing. If the order of Kipp's forty steps doesn't matter, for example, readers can pick and choose. If it does, the number of permutations is mind boggling: over a trillion trillion (8.15×10^{29} to be exact—we doubt he had time to test them all).

Fortunately for our purposes, the aspects of human experience we're concerned with are fundamentally nonlinear and iterative (chapter 3). We present the following program in what has seemed to us, and those we've worked with, as roughly logical. That said, once you've got a sense of the whole, feel free to jump around and even skip based on your own judgment and needs.

1 The Objective: Love the Journey

As noted in the last chapter, our search for purpose-feeling is an ingredient in our larger quest for happiness.

We've also observed that feeling purposeful has more in common with maintaining health than reaching a destination. It may sound exhausting to say WHY is a perpetual process of search, maintenance, and reevaluation. This helps explain the appeal of claims that we can discover our life's purpose and be done with it.

But would we say that of, say, eating? Imagine if a mad scientist developed a super meal that we could eat once and never have to eat again. Does that sound appealing? Isn't there pleasure in eating? Isn't there pleasure in discovering new things?

Those who promise or aim for a one-and-done solution put themselves at odds with how the world works. As physicists and Zen masters point out, everything happens in waves, from light and sound to our energy and emotions to weather systems and markets— even very slowly, the formation and dissolution of rocks. In most areas, perpetual satisfaction is as realistic a prospect as finding an ocean wave that crests and holds its position forever. Perpetual light or dark both blind us. Perpetual human happiness involves some variety, some sense of gain and loss; otherwise it's just a movie with no stakes, no plot, and no value.

So what exactly are we aiming for? Does having an impact, making a difference, changing the world look the same for everyone?

Most of us intuitively believe it's desirable to get to our target state as quickly and easily as possible, then stay there. If we could snap our fingers and feel purposeful, that sounds pretty good. Aside from speed, many assume that to achieve our best, we must aim to be the best.

We challenge that assumption. Not only does it have little in the way of foundation, unless you are selling a solution, but we've come to see it as counterproductive.

It may feel natural to want to live like those who have achieved outsize success and tell us this is the only way that they've experienced so far. But let's trace its implications. Someone who achieves early success doesn't necessarily mean they're living their best life. A Hollywood agent we know observes that clients who reach the top early in their careers are typically more fragile as people. "They've not been tested," she observes, "so they know who they are and who they are not." Likewise, does one experience more impact and fulfillment by achieving A-list status as the child of an A-lister—a "nepo baby"— or by making the B or C list on their own?

Once we've met our original success goal, the temptation is typically to hold that position instead of continuing to grow and discover. Whereas mastering the rise and fall of life's waves, continuing to expand our know-how is often a more fulfilling experience than worrying about losing ground.

Even if we're only seeking to be the best version of ourselves or to live our best life, what does that mean on a daily basis? How do we know when we're there? Would we even recognize (or be satisfied with) our best self when it arrives? We can't know we've overshot or ended up in the wrong place until we've gone there.

Thoughts of a single, ideal state are thus largely unhelpful on our quest to increased purpose-feeling. A better strategy is to stop worrying and learn to love the journey. What does this look like in practice? Focusing less on what we are doing or might achieve than on how we are getting there. When we commit to mindful discovery, we start to find that accumulating insight feels as rewarding as whatever we might do with it.

The alternative is a life where our sense of purpose and well-being are at the mercy of factors beyond our control, in other words, luck. A life in which purpose and well-being are attached (and thus limited) to a certain outcome is fleeting and unsatisfactory. And like the dog that caught the car, we have no idea what to do next.

This pattern is well illustrated in Brett Rapkin's 2020 documentary *The Weight of Gold*, which explores the fates of ex-Olympians.

Once these driven individuals find themselves on the other side of their life's goal, they feel a devastating loss of identify. As swimmer Michael Phelps, winner of a record twenty-three gold medals, puts it:

> *If your whole life was about building up to one race, one performance, or one event, how does that sustain everything that comes afterward? Eventually, for me at least, there was one question that hit me like a ton of bricks: Who was I outside of the swimming pool?*

Successful entrepreneurs often find themselves in the same place. Not entirely sure what they did right the first time, they're not sure how to repeat or find new goals. Some fritter away at least part of their fortunes trying to repeat their success (the Elon Musk-Twitter debacle comes to mind). Others retire from the world at a young age for fear of failure. At the opposite end of the spectrum, we've worked with owners leading businesses well beyond their intended retirement age, unable to let go for fear of losing themselves.

2 The Process: Think Lean (Like a Scientist)

Some may consider Louis Liebenberg's claim that humans are natural scientists off-putting. It conjures up images of carefully designed experiments conducted under tightly controlled conditions.

In borrowing his term, we simply mean that we are natural learners with an innate, if imperfect, sense of how to infer conclusions from experiences. Most human knowledge, from the languages we use, to the parts of the world we've explored, to products that make life easier—has been discovered outside of laboratories. Pure science has punched well above its weight in the last two centuries, notably in medicine and information technology. Still, it's no stretch to characterize much of what we do each day, especially at work, as "science by other means."

In few places is this better illustrated than the Lean school of product development that many view as Silicon Valley's greatest intellectual export. "Lean" does not mean doing things on the cheap— many practitioners have eye-watering budgets—but reducing waste in the innovation process. Its premise: even the most promising ideas we come up with at work are just that—ideas—and not necessarily as strong as they might seem on the whiteboard. New products and features should be treated not as almost certain successes— the way Coca-Cola once bet its brand on New Coke, one of the greatest product failures in history—but as guesses worth testing.

This means adapting the rigors of the scientific method to business with testable hypotheses, data gathering plans, and analysis in "minimum viable" (that is, minimally testable) releases.

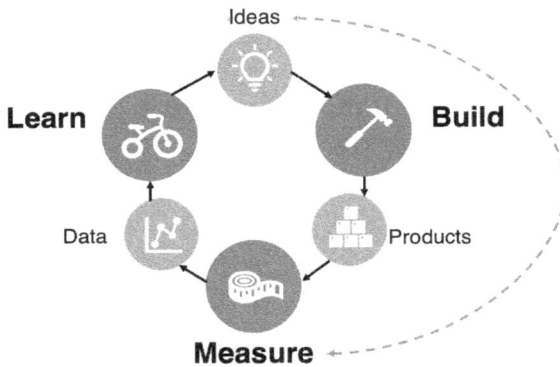

Exhibit 7.3: The Lean Learning Loop
Source: Eric Ries, Stephen Butler, and Karissa Price

This process creates the Lean Learning Loop (Exhibit 7.3). Each pass through it generates new knowledge, which either edges the competition right away or, more often, creates a basis for further attempts. Know-how is competitive advantage: the faster one can iterate, itself a form of knowledge or advantage, the faster one can increase it. This is not rocket science. But it is science, or at least an approximation thereof in the messy conditions of real life.

The Lean Learning Loop adapts well to individual WHY seeking. As an early client in this project remarked: "If Lean can help us find Product-Market Fit, why not Self-Impact Fit?" It enables us to better examine our personal hypotheses about why we are feeling purpose-deficient (using the Self-Impact Compass) and gain actionable self-insight. Here's what the modification looks like:

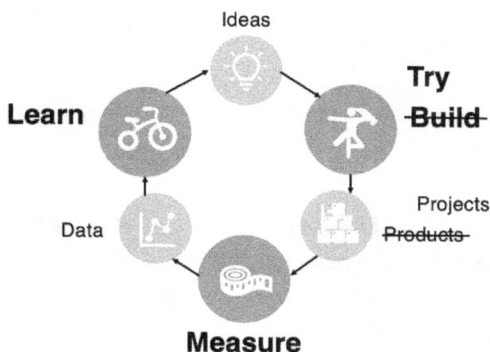

Exhibit 7.4: The Lean WHY Loop
Source: Eric Ries, Stephen Butler, and Karissa Price

To use this "Lean WHY Loop":

- Leverage the Self-Impact Compass to generate the *Ideas* you want to validate. (See the next section for more on this.)
- Self-assign *Projects* to undertake and test (e.g., seeking more responsibility, exploring other opportunities), making sure that results are measurable.
- *Measure* the results, even if simply a reflection of how they feel. (Objective measures are hard to come by here; don't let that stop you.)
- *Learn* from your *Data,* taking stock of your knowledge once you've been through the loop—repeat—and (per the last section) enjoy.

This process is all about mindful iteration, or what performance guru Geoff Colvin calls "deliberate practice." Know-how or skill is developed not simply by repetition but through systematic, goal-oriented repetition. One does not become a better basketball player by shooting hoops willy-nilly but by working on specific shots from specific distances and angles.

Closely associated with this "growth mindset," as psychologist

Carol Dweck calls it, is the view that we cannot learn without failure. If you succeed out the gate, you have no way of knowing if that was simply the result of good fit or if you do something else better. We can only discover fit by experiencing non-fit. Mindful failure is essential. NBA legend Michael Jordan once told an interviewer:

> *I've missed over 9,000 shots in my career. I've lost almost 300 games. Twenty-six times, I've been trusted to take the game-winning shot and missed. I've failed over and over in my career and that is why I succeed.*

3 The Starting Point: Use Boredom, Frustration, and Anxiety

A question we get from those keen to try their hand at Lean WHY Learning is, where do I begin?

Many self-diagnostics start with identifying where we're feeling pain. Pain is not just a signal something isn't working, but a clue where to focus. As Ray Dalio puts it: "Pain + Reflection = Progress.")

When our clients and teams feel WHY-deficient, they tend to report feeling one or more of these pain points:

- *Boredom*: lacking passion for what we're doing, the Drudge feeling.
- *Anxiety*: fear that our work is or may soon be beyond our capabilities, the Impostor feeling.
- *Frustration*: not being able to do what we want to do, the Dream feeling.

Once we pinpoint our pains—and thus our likely place on the Self-Impact Compass—the next step is undertaking Projects that test how they might be reduced.

Say you identify your primary pain at work as boredom (perhaps the most common). This has two basic flavors: work that is overly repetitive by nature or work that has become overly repetitive for us.

In the first scenario, our intuition is to start looking for something more interesting. Fair enough. But meanwhile, in the spirit of learning, we recommend what we call The Stanislavski Stratagem.

Konstantin Stanislavski was a legendary Soviet stage director who famously declared, "There are no small parts, only small actors." The sentiment is not entirely fair; there are certainly some very small jobs out there. But this is a helpful reminder that there's something to be learned from almost any job. Many leaders, including Amazon's Jeff Bezos, journalist Katie Couric, and President George W. Bush's Chief of Staff Andrew Card, once flipped burgers at McDonald's, later crediting the experience with teaching them much about efficiency, diligence, and customer experience.

If your job feels small, consider two tactics besides quitting: Grow it into something bigger, or see if it can be eliminated. You work not just for money, but to grow. Recruiters call this expanding your "skill balance sheet," or know-how that makes you more valuable in other jobs. Time is the one commodity that can't be created. Don't waste yours.

One of us once worked with a receptionist who persuaded her manager there weren't enough office visitors to warrant a full-time position. The marketing department, however, was swamped following a major product release. She helped clear the backlog, then left as an "efficiency expert" who had worked herself out of not one but two jobs. Today, she's a partner in a temp agency.

The other variant of boredom—work that has become repetitive to us—tends to occur later in our careers. The good news? By the time we feel this way, we've typically become skilled and/or senior enough to set ourselves new, more challenging goals, engaging others to work with us in the process, which is how this book started. Several mid-market CEOs we've worked with have found renewed passion simply by deciding to raise their company targets.

4 The Output: Learn Your Self

A 2005 survey of patent holders found that nearly half their discoveries had been the product not of intentional hypothesis testing, but accident. Many inventions solved problems investors weren't even aware of.

In the broader world of informal learning we're talking about, the rate of serendipitous discovery appears to be even higher.

Take note. We do not always need to be purposeful to live in purpose. We don't always have to walk around with a heavily stickied workbook, pressuring ourselves to think systematically. We can also enjoy the world without worrying about wasting time. This doesn't mean all experience is equally valuable—just a reminder that we don't need to be constantly calculating. Ideas may help, if only to focus our attention. But we do this naturally, without any special effort—that's why we need to respect our Passions.

Bottom line: the Discovery that leads to Know-How and Impact is less like studying for an exam than a trip to an unfamiliar city, where we lean on what we already know and our ability to acquire knowledge in order to navigate. In other words, once we've got the mindset and working model, Discovery is life. This is not a trite observation. Asked to explain the feeling of Zen enlightenment, master D.T. Suzuki observed, "It's just like everyday life, only two inches off the ground."

A helpful theme in Western thought may be traced to Socrates, who believed happiness required self-knowledge. This means appreciating what makes us different, the things we have to offer. We discover this by interacting with others, including the workplace.

Individuals we've worked with have found great value in self-assessment tools. None is a silver bullet. Collectively, however, such tools provide ways to understand our complex experience, navigate toward the middle of the Self-Impact Compass, even stumble upon one or more WHYs.

For starters, get to know your personal style. Use diagnostics such as the Myers-Briggs Type Indicator (MBTI), DiSC Profile, the Enneagram Personality Test, and the Predictive Index. These can help identify the roles and contexts where you may have the most impact with the least amount of energy, and why a job might feel exhausting or exhilarating.

Next, don't let your current job completely define your sense of the needs you can serve. Many skills required at work are different from those acquired at school or in life. Assess yours using tools such as Gallup's Clifton StrengthsFinder and the High5 Test.

Finally, broaden your passions with an interactive values tool such as www.personalvalu.es. Given the importance of empathy in problem-solving, value creation, and teamwork, take a few empathy tests. Note whether these are measuring cognitive empathy (our ability to imagine others' feelings), affective empathy (our tendency to share others' emotions), or both, like psychologist Simon Baron-Cohen's Empathy Quotient.

The results need not define us. Many find their MBTI and DiSC profiles evolve based on career demands. In high-paced environments, for example, you can become more focused on reaching conclusions than on gathering facts (more "Judging" than "Perceiving").

At the end of the day, tools are tools. Let them serve you, enhance your self-knowledge, understand your progress. Don't let them become objectives; there is no right Myers-Briggs profile. The things that resonate will stick. Don't worry about the rest.

5 The Lighthouse: Love Reality

Life and business coaches often encourage visualization for their clients, that is, picturing what one's best life might look like.

This can be risky, for the very reason Lean was invented: We simply don't have enough information to know what will work for us until we try. It's also hard to envision what a state we haven't experienced will look like, which seems to explain why Tony Robbins and others focus us on material things, like having "a bigger house, more money, and more vacations." That said, some kind of WHY visioning can be useful if approached with caution. This can help us better understand how to develop our resting road map—what success might look like not just in its final state but along the way. A thousand-mile journey starts with one step, as the Chinese proverb goes.

It's critical not to mistake our map for the journey, the recipe for the meal. Having a plan that makes the path easier does not mean the path will be easy.

This may sound like a marginal concern, particularly to those at earlier stages of their careers. History, however, is rife with stories of preconceptions blinding us: Many European explorers who expected to see mythical creatures like dragons and mermaids reported them in their journals.

The problem is no less pronounced in the modern workplace. Jim Collins found the danger of personal and corporate self-delusion so pronounced that he highlighted "reality-based thinking" as a key to corporate greatness.

In some contexts, like in a fading industry, facts may seem discouraging. Even worse, however, is pretending they aren't there, which delays necessary action. If Blockbuster hadn't lied to itself about how much consumers hated late fees, it could have become Netflix.

Embrace reality in three ways:

1. *Set realistic goals.* If you think you have what it takes to run a company, aim to lead one that's profitable and sustainable-already a bold, 20-to-1 shot—not the next Steve Jobs.* This does not preclude breakout success if you get lucky, but to assume great luck is to increase your risk of failure. As we heard one CEO tell her team, "Aim your arrow just above the target, not at the sky."

2. *Divide your vision into phases.* If you dream of running a company or disrupting an industry, understand and aim for steps along the way, like running a product team or disrupting a corporate practice. This is both good training and a way to confirm whether this vision is really for you.

3. *Focus.* When we choose to get good at something, we are choosing not to be as good at other things. That's okay: You can always back out if you find your specialty is not for you. But no one can be good at everything. As we've noted throughout the book, this world values specialization. There's nothing constructive about becoming a jack of all trades and master of none.

---

* Many have noted that if Theranos's Elizabeth Holmes had aimed a little lower, she might today be a great CEO of a smaller company, instead of a convicted fraudster.

Remember, learning builds your potential to have impact. You may not choose what you learn, but you can choose to value your learning or not.

Do not undervalue your experience. If it feels like you didn't make a dent today, if you can't see your path to impact, you are making a cumulatively invaluable impact on yourself just by seeking.

This isn't just getting closer to purpose. This is part of living it: an essential part of your WHY Iceberg. ☙

KEY TAKEAWAYS

1. Turning purpose into productivity growth and well-being means operationalizing empathy, which requires action and attitude shifts from managers and employees alike.
2. Employees can get their bearings with the Self-Impact Compass, a new purpose paradigm that points to WHY as an evolving feeling of Self-Impact, which is essentially a match between our skills, energies, and impact on others.
3. Finding direction through the Self-Impact Compass involves the alignment of three factors: WHERE we see our impact potential (our industry), WHAT we do every day (our role), and HOW we do it (our work environment).
4. We can use the Self-Impact Compass to follow these best practices:
   a. Start wherever you sense a problem. It's a nonlinear process, so you can't start in the "wrong" place.
   b. Prioritize your key move, from changing jobs to switching industries.
   c. Approach changes as experiments, not truths.
   d. Target progress, not perfection: WHY is a journey.
   e. Dig into your personal drivers.
   f. Use self-assessment tools to better understand yourself.
   g. If lost, focus on your WHAT. Your role and responsibilities are easiest to change.
   h. Embrace "small jobs," meaning learn from whatever role you are in, however limited.
   i. Remember that whatever you do, you're learning. And learning always has an impact on YOU.

CHAPTER 8

What Managers Must Do

"We cannot make anything grow. But we can foster environments where things want to grow."

MARCUS BRIDGEWATER

THE NEW CEO, "FRED," WAS NOT HAPPY. Earlier that year, his family-owned commercial construction firm, "BuildCo," had published its first purpose statement.

Fred's father, the former CEO turned chairman, was no fan of what he saw as management fads. He'd warned that the whole effort would be a waste of time and money.

Looking to make his own mark, Fred had plowed ahead. He'd hired a marketing agency to run the process. His senior leadership team had been interviewed, along with customers, suppliers, and employees.

To Fred's delight, the organization quickly rallied around the resulting mission. "We Build Proud Owners" aligned with BuildCo's customer service philosophy, reflected the research, and sounded fresh. Even his dad grudgingly agreed it could have been worse.

Six months later, however, Fred was struggling to make sense of another BuildCo first: its employee survey.

Managers at all levels expressed strong satisfaction with the words now inscribed on the company's workwear, scoring it an average 4.6 out of 5.

Yet the share who said they got value from the mission at least once a week? A paltry nine percent.

"So everybody loves this thing, but nobody uses it?" Fred fumed to an adviser. "What are we supposed to do about that?!"

"Maybe," said the adviser, "we should use it."

The comment was not meant to be glib. The adviser was just highlighting the circularity of Fred's problem, which a recent Bain & Company survey had found to be far from uncommon (chapter 2), while underlining a simple truth: Even the greatest missions do not put themselves to work.

It was no surprise that BuildCo's leadership liked the mission. They had found great value in the articulation process. The idea that its services should produce a specific emotional benefit for clients was a powerful, actionable insight.

What they had yet to figure out, however, was how to operationalize such insight as a source of ongoing value creation. There's only so much magic one can get from words alone. As Netflix's Reed Hastings points out, Enron inscribed "Integrity" on its walls even as it engaged in history-making fraud.

Managers and employees need to *use* purpose statements, not just admire them.

But what does that actually mean?

THE PRINCIPLES OF BUSINESS PURPOSE

Let's recap what we've learned so far about how purpose delivers value at various levels:

1. The purpose of business as a practice is to solve human problems (chapter 4).

2. The purpose of companies is to lower transaction costs in a specific area (effectively, "solution costs") by accumulating know-how and productive assets (chapter 5).
3. The purpose of employees is to combine company know-how and assets with personal empathy and insight to innovate and have impact (chapter 6).

To understand what leaders can do to make this happen, we must add a few more principles, which we'll elaborate in this chapter:

4. The purpose of managers is to fit, engage, and align employee efforts.
5. The purpose of senior leaders is to ensure management consistency and accountability.
6. The purpose of purpose itself is to focus and facilitate all of the above.

For reference, here is a visualization:

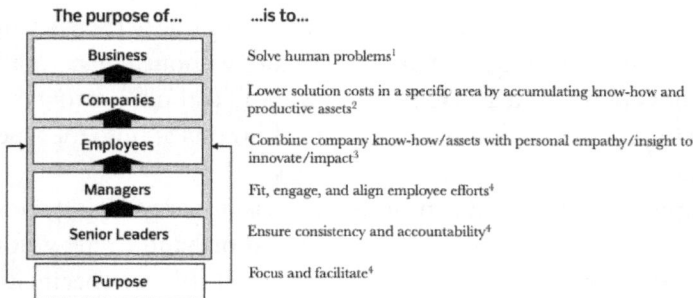

The purpose of...	...is to...
Business	Solve human problems[1]
Companies	Lower solution costs in a specific area by accumulating know-how and productive assets[2]
Employees	Combine company know-how/assets with personal empathy/insight to innovate/impact[3]
Managers	Fit, engage, and align employee efforts[4]
Senior Leaders	Ensure consistency and accountability[4]
Purpose	Focus and facilitate[4]

Sources: 1.Eric Beinhocker, Nicholas Georgescu-Roegen, 2.Ronald Coase, 3.Adam Smith, 4.Authors

Exhibit 8.1 The principles of business purpose
Source: Stephen Butler and Karissa Price

A PROGRAM OF PURPOSE-DRIVEN MANAGEMENT: AIM

We've experimented with various ways of turning these principles into a holistic program. What we've come to call the AIM approach offers a strong combination of accessibility and effectiveness.

The AIM steps

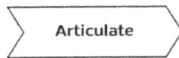

Articulate	Implement	Measure
1: Create a "Rallying WHY" Define the impact objective at the organization and team level	*3: Specify Individual ACCOUNTABILITIES* Ensure everyone understands how their role fits in the whole	*5: Track LEADERSHIP Effectiveness* Provide metrics and development for managers
2: Make CULTURE Explicit Define HOW the WHY is to be achieved	*4: Provide Impact FEEDBACK Loops* Help employees feel their impact in a timely manner	*6: Monitor Implementation CONSISTENCY* Track compliance and effectiveness of all the above

Exhibit 8.2 Overview of the AIM program
Source: Stephen Butler and Karissa Price

Articulate Purpose

Peter Drucker was right. Just as it's hard to win a game without a pan or guide a group through unfamiliar territory without a map, it's all but impossible to get teams to perform without communicating the type of impact that is required of each, and how this fits into the type of impact the organization wants to have.

Purpose statements like missions and visions are rallying cries for teams— and, as a client once put it, the "shorthand strategy" for an organization (see Step 1, below). They must balance specificity and actionability with inspiration and memorability.

It's not enough to know just *what* we're all trying to do, however. Everyone needs to know the broad strokes of *how*. Organizations must specify their target culture, including the ideal modes of collaboration and communication—i.e., what should go on inside and outside of meetings—and the behaviors that lead its members to be hired, promoted, and dismissed.

Implement Purpose

Just being aware of a team's high-level WHY and HOW does not provide sufficient information (or capability) to perform well. Managers must provide support and mechanisms to guide behavior on the ground.

This starts with detailed descriptions of job and team objectives, tying back to corporate priorities. It continues with mechanisms to ensure all get the feedback they need to know they're making progress—to help employees "hear themselves play" (per client Anika's analogy in chapter 6). Once these tools become the locus for constructive, ongoing conversations about output and impact at all levels, they become sustainable.

Measure Purpose

We're still only dealing with ideas, not truths: guesses or hypotheses as to what will create value. To know whether they are working, they need to be tracked and learned from.

Even the best-intentioned implementation of purpose can be derailed by factors discussed in chapter 6, such as the toxic boss who elevates their personal agenda above the whole, or the narrow-minded one who focuses only on partial metrics. It's up to the managers of managers—senior leaders—to snuff out such behaviors by focusing managers' attention on the right priorities and paying attention to what's going on.

Employees look to senior leadership to demonstrate that the WHY is real by consistently holding their bosses accountable. When the day-to-day walk doesn't match the talk, trust erodes—and the organization is worse off than it started.

ARTICULATE
PRACTICE 1: CREATE A "RALLYING WHY"

Define the impact objective at the organization and team level
Primary tool: SASSY visions, missions, and values statements
Practical leaders often dismiss the articulation of WHY as unneces-

sary. "Isn't it obvious?" we've heard many clients say before they start.

It isn't. This is why the father of modern management (Drucker) placed so much stock in the practice. No team can deliver effectively if it doesn't understand what "deliver" and "effectively" means.

Enter the purpose statement. As a client once put it:

> *No middle manager or employee is going to read, let alone remember, an eighty-page strategy. We don't even try. If we want them aligned, we need a "strategic shorthand" they can grasp. That's where I see the mission and vision come in.*

Yet another client observed:

> *A good WHY is a rallying WHY.*

Articulation is a necessary starting point for engaging teams. It's also an advisable periodic ritual, for reasons we'll get to.* But not all articulation is created equal. There are best practices.

The form of purpose statement varies. Fifty years down the road Peter Drucker set us on, common practice has settled on three parts: the vision, mission, and values, which are interdependent and often muddled. Of the competing definitions that have sprung up, we've found the following most helpful:

- The VISION is a *broad*, long-term take on the organization's WHY: the way it would like to impact the world. This part typically follows the form, *"We envision a world in which X becomes a reality."* Many include the company's place in that world, and specify a time horizon. This can also help point to how a company might evolve from where it is today. An example is TMX Group, which began life as the Toronto Stock Exchange, a cooperative owned by Canadian trading firms, before going

---

* So long as we don't get carried away. Yahoo! notoriously published no fewer than twenty-four missions in its twenty-one-year history, which did little to keep it from falling apart.

public in 2002. Thereafter, its vision was to bring "dial-tone reliability to high-frequency financial transaction platforms," allowing it to spread its wings into new data services and asset classes, including derivatives and energy.

- The MISSION is a company's core statement of the WHY: the *specific* impact the company intends to have in accelerating the vision, starting right now. *"Our purpose is to do Y so that X happens."* Many incorporate the vision or present it side by side. TMX's mission is to "power capital and commodity markets with client-centric, technology-driven global solutions" so that it can "make markets better and empower bold ideas."
- VALUES amount to the organization's HOW: the principles guiding the way its people interact with each other and the world. (Clearly this needs to be aligned with the vision. It makes no sense to value wild risk-taking if the impact is reliability.) TMX's values are to be client-centric and courageous while building and maintaining trust—a solid guide to action.*

The output of such exercises can be rote, uninspired, and even counterproductive. Scott Adams's cartoon cubicle dweller Dilbert famously defined "mission statement" as "a long, awkward sentence that demonstrates management's inability to think clearly."

How can we create them in a way that inspires action and pride rather than mockery? Bad writing, that is, writing that's unclear, dull or, as Gen Zs say, "cringe"— can be worse than none.†

We've identified best practices for the rallying mission that can be remembered with the mnemonic, SASSY. A SASSY mission is

---

* Recently, some companies have taken to articulating a "purpose statement" over and above the vision, mission and values. We believe that if the vision and mission are well constructed, a purpose statement is likely to be redundant. However, if you find yourself struggling with the vision/mission distinction—or it simply feels forced—a single purpose statement is a perfectly respectable alternative or complement.

† For this reason, even Apple, a company that's often held up as the poster child for purpose, has gone for long stretches without publishing any kind of purpose statement at all.

- *Short*: ideally less than twenty-five words, thus memorable;
- *Actionable*: a rallying cry for employees, not shareholders or customers;
- *Special*: describing the company uniquely, not the industry (differentiation is the essence of strategy);
- *Sincere*: something leadership is demonstrably committed to, and sounds like them; and
- *Young (or Fresh)*: avoiding clichés and familiar phrasing that sounds tired and uninspiring.

Consider two versions of an online shoe retailer's mission. Before:

"At OnlineShoes.com, we are passionate about helping our customers find the perfect pair of shoes to fit their unique style and needs. We strive to provide a seamless online shopping experience, offering a wide selection of high-quality shoes from top brands at competitive prices. Our mission is to not only meet but exceed our customers' expectations by delivering exceptional customer service and making their shoe shopping experience enjoyable and convenient." (Source: ChatGPT-4)

After becoming SASSY:

"Deliver WOW." (Source: Zappos, a subsidiary of Amazon.)

A good purpose statement is one employees don't just accept, but repeat and find actionable. Zappos's is a prime example.

The articulation process does not end at the corporate level, especially for large companies. If frontline managers and employees are expected to figure out their implications for themselves, confusion and disagreement will abound. The next step is, thus, to "waterfall" the overall purpose statements to the divisional and team level (a bit like Sinek et al.'s "nested WHYs," but in top down, not bottom up).

Team missions or charters articulate the specific role that teams play in delivering the overall mission. Zappo's accounts payable department, for example, may "deliver WOW" by paying suppliers much faster than the competition, and/or with more user-friendly record keeping.

Building a team charter involves:

- *Identifying* the team's primary "customer." This can be an external customer. Often, it's another team within the organization whose work depends on its deliverables;
- *Specifying* how it wants to impact those customers and perhaps the organization more broadly (the team vision, e.g., to help the company become known for its customer service);
- *Specifying* what it intends to do to advance that vision (the team mission, for example, to surprise customers with attention to detail); and
- *Detailing* how it intends to operate as a unit (the values, such as, "we're a jazz band," "we have OCD," "we're mad scientists"—all real examples we've seen).

When purpose statements come alive, their value is unmistakable. Consider an example that has stood the test of time. Walmart is the world's largest private employer, with 2.3 million associates around the world. Founded by retailer Sam Walton in 1962, its vision is "to build a better world—helping people live better and renew the planet while building thriving, resilient communities." Its mission: "to help consumers save money so they can live better lives." This is reflected in the company's values, a code of employee conduct: Service to the customer, *Respect* for the individual, striving for *Excellence*, and acting with *Integrity*.

During the COVID-19 pandemic, with inflation rapidly rising, the head of food merchandising exhorted the company's purchasers weekly to keep costs down for customers. Employees felt proud of the impact they had by keeping groceries affordable for struggling customers. This paid off in multiple forms of value: Walmart grew market share. Its stock price rose despite initial Wall Street criticism. Employee engagement soared.

PRACTICE 2: MAKE CULTURE EXPLICIT

Align execution by defining HOW the WHY is to be achieved
Primary tool: culture decks

Inspiring words, even at the team level, can leave a lot open to interpretation. "Deliver WOW" may help inspire a redesigned unboxing experience. But what about a remote work policy?

Before companies can begin to live a WHY, another level of articulation is needed: the HOW.

Within a decade of founding Netflix, as the company approached its thousandth hire, CEO Reed Hastings recognized a new challenge. Employees understood the company's direction. As new hires came on board, however, productivity was declining and turnover rising. What was missing was a shared sense of how the company was different from other employers, what made it work at its best, what kind of employee experience and career path was to be expected.

Hastings's solution was an innovative tool that's since been adopted by thousands of companies: the Culture Deck.

"Culture," as Tim Ferriss laments (chapter 3), is a much-used and misunderstood term. Practically, it is a set of behaviors expected of employees in day-to-day work. When these are followed, frictions and disagreements are reduced; energies can be expended on getting work done, rather than debating how. If some are working sixty-hour weeks while others are barely hitting forty, conflict and misalignment are likely to follow.

A culture deck is a guide to action for managers and employees at all levels, detailing what a company's values mean in practice:

- The behaviors and attitudes that get individuals hired, promoted, and dismissed. For example, is risk-taking and innovation favored (as among the "mad scientist" team referenced in the previous section), or compliance and thoroughness (as among the "OCD" one)?
- How meetings work, and how communication is expected to

work both in and outside of them. Consider: Are meetings intended to build consensus, solicit feedback, or simply communicate decisions already made?

- Where and when work is to be done—at home or at work and at what hours?
- How values apply in making decisions, particularly difficult ones. Does client-centric mean putting a client's profitability first, or simply taking it into account?

At the end of the day, as Hastings put it, a culture deck is intended to replace "nice-sounding values" that often get tacked on to formal values by well-meaning managers. For Netflix, this meant replacing claims such as "We're like a family" (which implies helping struggling performers get better) with "We're like a professional sports team" (which better reflected its practice of packaging out laggards quickly).

A good culture deck helps explains what pithy and, thus, high-level purpose statements mean in practice. This starts at the top. The idea is not to reflect how the company works today, rather how leadership would like it to work, albeit in keeping with Lean principles; that is, not expecting to be 100 percent right but to track reception, gather employee input, and iterate as necessary.

The contents generally include an explanation of what a culture deck is (less necessary as they become more common), a statement of the values, and examples of applying them in common situations (from holding meetings to giving feedback to making hires).

A culture deck does more than guide. It democratizes articulation and reflection, driving engagement and producing real data on how a company's purpose statements are actually being received.

Now we're starting to really bring purpose to life. Unfortunately, many purpose "implementations" stop here, waiting for the magic to happen.

Actually, we're just getting started.

IMPLEMENT
PRACTICE 3: SPECIFY INDIVIDUAL ACCOUNTABILITIES

Ensure everyone understands how their role fits in the whole Primary tool: ARC (Accountabilities/Resources/ Consequences) agreements

Implementing purpose at work means providing individuals and teams with the support they need to do what the articulations ask. This starts with taking purpose down to the individual level. Each employee must understand:

- The impact they are personally *accountable* for (deliverables they're accountable for and the "customer" for each);
- The *resources* they require in order to deliver (tools and training to do the job, inputs they receive from others to process, feedback on their output from their manager and others, plus development support); and
- The career development and compensation *consequences* they can expect from good or weak performance.

An effective tool for instituting all this is a formal yet living accountability contract between individual employees and managers. We've found such agreements to be incredibly powerful in aligning collective and individual purpose to produce favorable results. So much great work in organizations falls apart in the absence of clarity and tracking on such points.

Accountability contracts can be more or less detailed. The model championed by industrial psychologists Bruce Klatt, Shaun Murphy, and David Irvine has seven parts. This can be a lot to keep track of. We've achieved traction with a streamlined, three-part model that aligns with the above bullets and the acronym ARC: Accountabilities, Resources, and Consequences.

An ARC agreement is an evergreen tool to keep employees on

track, remind managers of their support obligations, and set an agenda for regular "support meetings," which focus less on individual performance assessment than collaborative troubleshooting. A good ARC details not only the impact the team requires from the individual, but the impact the individual aims to have on themselves, in other words, the skills they are looking to develop and career goals they aim to pursue.

A critical feature is specificity. An ARC clarifies what managers often take for granted, and what employees are often confused about: what a role's daily, weekly, and longer-term impact looks like, and how that impact can be measured. If the employee's core accountability is to generate sales leads, their progress can be measured in terms of number of leads generated as well as quality (how often leads turn into customers). If their personal goals include getting more senior-level engagement with customers and internal stakeholders, that can be measured as well. If the job as structured doesn't allow for this, the boss can consider if this might change, or the employee can begin working towards another role that does.

An ARC's most essential quality is to be, like any agreement, a two-way street. A manager cannot require accountabilities of a report without providing resources, including an often-overlooked one we're about to elaborate, and reasonable consequences.

IMPLEMENT PRACTICE 4: PROVIDE IMPACT FEEDBACK LOOPS

Help employees feel their own impact in a timely manner
Primary tools: Personal Dashboards, Peer Recognition

Musicians can't perform well if they can't hear their instruments. Likewise, employees can't perform—let alone feel purposeful and engaged—if they can't tell what difference their work makes.

If building workplace "amps" was easy, managers would all be doing it, and our problems with WHY would not loom as large. The challenge can be captured in one word: data. Identifying, collecting, and rendering in good time measures that meaningfully represent an employee's impact is hard.

The key to getting around this lies in a Lean mindset: not expecting success right out of the gate, but approaching the challenge in a spirit of invention and iteration.

Before considering examples we've seen work, it's essential to note that the feedback metrics we're talking about are intended to provide timely information for the individual to use in optimizing their performance, not for managers to make compensation or promotion decisions.

As Daniel Pink points out, employees place a high value on autonomy. A race driver's accountability is to win races, not optimize dashboard readings. The latter are there to help them manage the vehicle and, if necessary, get support from their pit crew, not to determine if they won the "right" way. Likewise, if impact feedback mechanisms become less a personal gauge than a managerial monitoring system, they will diminish autonomy and reduce engagement.

School studies suggest the best learning comes from informal measurements like quizzes; as soon as the mark counts toward a grade, anxiety levels rise and learning diminishes. Likewise, employees learn and develop most effectively when they can get feedback that does not have financial or career consequences. They're happy to be judged on a board presentation, but they're happier to get feedback on drafts from their manager and others along the way.

Falling afoul of this principle can be devastating. If an individual or team stands to lose by seeking help on a weak metric, they won't ask for help, or they'll try to conceal or distort the metric. No one wins.

With this in mind, let's turn to feedback practices we've found effective.

Dashboards

Call centers have long used dashboards to help teams understand their real-time performance. They display how many calls have been handled during the shift, how many are waiting to be served, average hold times and so on. Shift managers can see where backlogs are mounting and call in or send home resources as necessary. Individual agents can also track their own call handling and satisfaction rates, comparing them with targets and averages.

Until recently, most jobs have not supported such precise and timely tracking, largely because apples-to-apples data gathering seems impossible. In law, for example, residential real estate agreements might be fairly standard, but the size and complexity of commercial agreement ranges widely. How can a lawyer track her own efficiency, let alone efficacy?

Tech companies specialize in turning seemingly intractable real-world activities into manageable digital flows, and they've begun to step into the breach. Software engineers have long used project management software to track individual tasks, output, dependencies, and efficiency. Productivity platforms like ClickUp and Monday have retooled these for general users. These tools tend to focus primarily on task completion rates as opposed to more meaningful impacts, such as skill development and external/internal customer satisfaction. But they can also help lawyers track their activity by standard units like word and page, as well as other qualities like deal value, rather than just "deals."

Yet the measures that can be made this way are often not the most meaningful. A salesperson may care about the length of their calls, but they care more about dimensions like client satisfaction. An analyst wants to know how various readers assess the quality of their reports. And so on.

Our teams have had great success capturing such things using what might be termed "semi-objective measures": subjective assessments that use an objective set of criteria. A sales call can be assessed not simply as effective or ineffective, but by specific factors that an individual might even observe of themselves, from following specific best practices to achieving specific goals, such as a follow-up commitment. This follows in the footsteps of the widely used Capability Maturity Model (CCM) developed at the US Department of Defense in the 1980s, which assesses competencies using a predefined, five-level scale (Exhibit 8.3).

Scale	Definition
1 - Non-existent	Practice, tool or process nonexistent
2 - Ad-hoc	Some aspects of the capability are being applied, only in an inconsistent fashion and often with poor results. Application is ad-hoc, in reaction to events, with no defined process.
3 - Defined and repeatable	Processes are documented, allowing a standard execution of the task when applied. These activities occur on a fairly regular basis and are subject to some degree of improvement over time.
4 - Managed and measurable	Processes are adopted across the organization and rigorously applied. They are aligned with the company strategy and objectives. Impact is evaluated through performance indicators.
5 - Optimized	The capability is fully deployed and is continuously improved in a formal sense. It can be rated as best-in-class.

Exhibit 8.3: The Capability Maturity Model
Source: US Department of Defense

Some managers seek to integrate semi-objective measures into customer relationship management (CRM) or business intelligence (BI) software, like Salesforce CRM or Microsoft's Power BI. These can be complicated, however, and the incremental value is often not worth the effort to start. Better to experiment first with a good "sandbox" in which to develop a sense of role- and team-specific requirements: an Excel workbook or Google Sheet (a spreadsheet), populated manually as agreed between manager and employee.

Strong personal dashboards include something like a personal journal, whereby the employee can capture their own learning and Self-Impact, such as:

- *Review* (the top three-five for each for previous period)
  - Wins
  - Lessons learned
  - Lessons Learned for the team/organization
  - Skills acquired
  - Plan (the top three-five for the next period)
- *Plan*

- Work Targets
- Skill Development Targets

We cannot stress enough how much *personal dashboards must be separated from performance assessment.* When these become conflated, the dashboard becomes less a tool to drive learning and intrinsic engagement than a means of persuading a manager to give extrinsic rewards. Or worse, they can be a weapon bad bosses might use to hold employees back, as a consequence for learning on the job.

Peer Recognition

Managers have long sought to motivate employees with something other than pay and promotion for obvious reasons: The former is costly and the latter not always possible.

The track record of a popular solution that has stepped into this breach, employee rewards programs, is mixed. Some may be motivated by the prospect of a day off or new headphones. Most find such schemes faintly ridiculous: The prize value doesn't compare with the effort required to earn them, and/or they invite colleagues' mockery.

Recently, however, a new solution has begun to complement and even replace such programs. Peer recognition systems like Bonusly and Kudos are digital platforms whereby employees are awarded points not just by their managers, but by colleagues. All receive periodic point allocations they can use to thank or recognize others for good work. While these can often be redeemed for prizes, many firms have dumped the idea. Employees often value the points more than anything they might trade them for; they don't crave the headphones, but they do the recognition.

Peer recognition turns out to be a remarkably strong proxy for personal impact. Commonly, employees give points to applaud work that has clear impact, on themselves, the team, or others. The more recognition a recipient gets, the more they are aware of their impact, and the more purposeful or engaged they feel. Such feedback is especially resonant with young employees that have grown up in a world of social media, where every picture, thought, and post is instantly rewarded with "likes" and "shares." Companies that have implemented peer recognition systems have drastically increased their Net Promoter Scores (the share of employees who recommend their employer over those who warn others away) or Great Place to Work scores (the share who would describe their workplace this way)—often leading their sectors.

Some industrial psychologists have raised concerns that such systems might become popularity contests or "sociograms," where point transfers reflect an individual's charisma rather than impact. Most platforms have found such risks are manageable: Points can be restricted to explicitly designated accountabilities and team goals, for example. Rationales can be required, providing additional feedback. Points can be "popularity adjusted," shifting the focus from absolute point levels to month-to-month changes—and so on.

Peer recognition is only a proxy for impact, much the way one's weight is only a proxy of physical health. Like bathroom scales, however, such systems are accessible, easy to use, and capable of generating real-time data. They effectively boil many variables down to a single number, with minimal workflow interruption. Thanks to the Q12 survey, managers understand personal recognition to be a direct driver of engagement, yet we've long lacked the technology to integrate its practice and measure into normal workflow.

Mindfully implemented, however, today's systems have the potential to be well-managed workplaces' most powerful individual "amps."

MEASURE
PRACTICE 5: TRACK LEADERSHIP EFFECTIVENESS

Provide metrics and development support for managers
Primary tool: Leadership Competency Models
As with any initiative, there's only one way to understand the impact

of purpose practices on performance: Measure it.

Many managers assume such benefits should be evident. If the idea is to increase productivity and profitability, why not focus on productivity and profitability?

The challenge: Make such financial measures full of "noise" from other factors. Market conditions may pressure prices and margins, for example, but that doesn't mean a purpose program rolled out simultaneously isn't helping.*

In this light, we've found it helpful to track three intermediary measures: employee engagement, leadership effectiveness, and real productivity.

Employee Engagement

In performance terms, engagement is manifested in two ways above all: 1) employees' investment of discretionary effort, which shows up in hours worked, time usage, and productivity (see next section), and 2) loyalty, which results in lower turnover rates.

These jump over a lot of intermediate steps and may be influenced by outside factors. Deeper, more actionable understanding can be had through polling employees, either by directly asking how engaged they feel or, what researchers favor, through indirect surveys such as the Gallup Q12, which digs into the moving parts (see chapter 3).

The challenge with thorough surveys is that they can become exhausting, even alienating to employees if done too frequently ("Didn't we just do this?"). A powerful and increasingly popular alternative is the pulse survey: a brief, sometimes single-question poll that measures different aspects of the employee experience. Pulses are relatively easy to conduct, noninvasive, and quick to generate results. They are often found to be fun and even inspiring for respondents ("My company cares enough to ask me my opinion every week,

---

* We repeatedly witnessed such confusion during the pandemic. It may have been a good idea to focus on engagement while employees were being laid off or sent to work from home, but the results could not be taken as typical.

without taking up my time"). If engagement has risen or slipped after implementing a peer recognition system, for example, management is immediately aware of where it needs to dig deeper.

Anonymity and convenience are key. Metric gathering should not distract from work, give employees the impression they're under constant scrutiny, or seem like a waste of time. To provide useful feedback, employees must feel confident that their opinions won't impact them negatively. For smaller teams of less than ten, manager check-ins with individual members are likely to be more revealing and constructive.

In-depth surveys can be helpful, but only when conducted sparingly. Participation tends to be lower and comments more cryptic, especially in low-engagement environments. If results are ambiguous, chances are you have an issue with psychological safety, meaning employees suspect that speaking up will have negative personal consequences—and that needs to be addressed first.* Other means of tracking engagement may work based on the nature of the situation :

- *Time Surveys.* Ask employees to track how much time they've spent on specific tasks in a given week, such as talking to customers, brainstorming, or handling emails. This isn't easy. Improve results by providing a limited list to pick from and conducting each survey with a big enough pool (e.g., at the company or divisional level) to ensure anonymity.
- *Indirect Engagement Measures.* Track other indicators of engagement, from absenteeism to town hall and suggestion box participation and how full the office is at 9 a.m. and 5 p.m. (or 8 a.m. and 6 p.m.) .
- *Poll Dependents/Customers.* Survey those who are dependent on the team's work (its customers) to gauge satisfaction with quality, timeliness, and so on, using a semi-objective, CMM-type scale for comparability (Exhibit 8.3).
- *Turnover and Exit Interviews.* There is often no greater source

---

* Psychological safety is the perception among employees that it's acceptable to take risks, question, and express candid opinions without fear of repercussion.)

of insight than the comments of a disgruntled customer or departing employee. These don't need to be taken at face value; often the value is in the interpretation discussion. The larger the organization, the more meaningful such data can be. Smaller organizations need to consider these over longer time frames.

Whatever measures you choose, don't begin tracking until you're prepared to weigh and act on the results. Asking employees or customers to invest their time and insights and then doing nothing is not just pointless but harmful. No one wants to do work that isn't valued; if not, future participation may plummet.

Leadership Effectiveness

As interesting as outputs like sales per representative can be, understanding the drivers, like the number and nature of sales calls, is typically more illuminating and actionable. In this spirit, some companies have shifted their survey focus from engagement (an output) to the driver that lies within most immediate control: leadership effectiveness.

According to Gallup, 75 percent of the reasons people cite for leaving a job—the ultimate disengagement!—are factors under a manager's control.

This makes a leader's competence a critical factor in the success of any team. This not only helps a manager or their superiors understand why team engagement is rising or falling because it calls attention to leadership practices that can be actively improved.

There are many tools available in this regard. Engagement surveys like we've just described or more specific 360 surveys that ask for individual manager feedback are both options. Their downside, however, particularly for a struggling manager, can be to reinforce negative perceptions.

A better approach can be to use managerial self-assessments with a semi-objective component. These ask questions about specific behaviors that don't obviously add up to strength or weakness. A tool some of our clients have found effective is The Leadership Circle, a multidimensional self-assessment akin to a Myers-Briggs or DiSC, which gives respondents a sense of how their current skills align with their career aspirations.

The key to improving leadership effectiveness comes down to what managers do with the findings.

Developing leadership is a learning process, and good learning, as we've discussed, requires the permission to fail, psychological safety, and radical candor. In this spirit and given what we've discussed about employee feedback tools, companies with strong general leadership scores often exclude leadership competence assessments from compensation formulas. They base the latter solely on outcomes, which can include people targets like engagement but are not directly tied to skill development. Identifying one's own leadership needs are consequenced not with less money but additional coaching and training.

If only someone had thought to do the same for Henderson's almost-stellar manager Joe (chapter 6).

Real Productivity

Managers need to keep an eye on productivity itself. This, for many, is the point of the entire purpose exercise.

Many are surprised to discover this can be tricky. Various factors that have nothing to do with purpose, engagement, or leadership can raise or lower productivity measures.

Most significant is pricing. Policymakers' preferred measure is output per hour, so it makes sense to track at a macroeconomic level. For individual firms and teams, however, this can be misleading. Why? Because output per hour is made up of price per unit times units produced per hour, which move independently. Nominal productivity can, thus, rise when operational productivity is falling.

This isn't just theory. In the post-pandemic boom, as companies rushed to recruit new hires, many saw nominal productivity rise (owing to inflation) even as average hourly production dipped (owing to worker inexperience). Many organizations looked more productive on paper than they really were.

The solution is to track what economists call real productivity, or, productivity adjusted for changes in costs or revenue per unit. This can be strictly calculated through a company's supply chain management (SCM) systems, which tracks the flow of goods from procurement through to delivery. A less formal calculation can be used in nonmanufacturing situations by maintaining rough measures of "units delivered per hour worked," where units can be hours, sales calls, proposals, and so forth.

For some, this raises a second problem: What are our "units delivered"? This is relatively straightforward in functions where standardized outputs (sales, signups, customer satisfaction) correlate roughly with inputs (calls, proposals, lead times). It's harder for teams that produce output of naturally varying size (e.g., deals, legal agreements, consulting recommendations) or operate as cost centers in an organization. Such situations require creativity to define trackable outputs, leaning on specific work product (page of legal or consulting advice) or semiobjective/CMM-type measures around quality or customer satisfaction.

But rest assured: Something can always be tracked.

MEASURE
PRACTICE 6: MONITOR
IMPLEMENTATION CONSISTENCY

Track compliance and effectiveness of all the above
Primary tool: Pulse Surveys

The factor most likely to lead to failure in a purpose implementation—and to leave teams worse off than they started—is management's failure to match walk and talk.

No one is quicker than employees to notice when an organization's principles are not being followed by its leaders, most commonly when inconsistent behavior in management ranks is tolerated. Other efforts to promote purpose look insincere. Trust is lost. Engagement plummets. Integrity refers to the parts of a thing holding it together. Lose consistency, and organizations literally disintegrate.

Senior leaders often contribute to the problem and fail to recognize its dangers because they overestimate the amount of work required to fix middle management failings, and underestimate the negative impact on the rest of the organization.

For some, the program outlined here may seem like a simple to-do list. Get seven of eight right, assuming roughly equal weighting, and they'll still be punching around an A or A-minus, right? Then, if there are exceptions, like a frontline manager failing to respect the ARC framework, it's easy to find excuses not to communicate with staff, such as, this is complex, a work in progress, we'll clean up when we're done.

In fact, if a leadership team fails to deliver or communicate on even a single element, it will be scoring closer to zero. What look, from above, like independent practices, are, on the ground, a single experience. The elements of a purpose implementation are not additive, but multiplicative. Score poorly on one element, say, commit to engagement surveys but don't share or act on the results, and the whole program fails.

In short, the mission needs to be strong, the vision meaningful. Culture decks and ARC agreements must be aligned and actionable. Individual feedback must be provided and development supported. Managers should be assessed and held accountable on their commitment to the above.

If not, employees are nobody's fools. They will respond in natural, human fashion by disengaging and heading for the door.

A case study powerfully illustrates this. A software company we worked with had a high-performing, well-liked CEO committed to diversity, equity, inclusion, and belonging (DEIB) principles. The firm rolled out an employee campaign, "We All Belong," to foster conversations and improve DEIB metrics at all levels.

When a division needed a new leader, the company hired a new leader who claimed to share these principles. She inherited a seven-person management team, including four people of color.

During her first year, however, three of those individuals left, along with a half-dozen Latino and Black employees, together representing over a quarter of the division. They resigned individually over time, each deciding they did not belong in their new leader's new culture.

Among remaining employees, regardless of ethnicity, morale tumbled. Continued DEIB enthusiasm from the CEO and HR was undermined by the resignations and remaining employees' own experiences. Disillusionment with the company and CEO rose. Productivity fell. In one exit interview, a once-rising star called out the employee campaign: "Well, *I* don't belong."

The CEO was baffled. The problem was just one leader in an organization that had hundreds. "She's new," he insisted to an adviser. "We can bring her along. Plus, all our other divisions are doing fine."

The adviser was reminded of an old joke about a Parisian chef, who shocks a visitor by throwing live lobsters into boiling water.

"Isn't that painful?" the visitor asks.

"They're used to it," says the chef. "I've been doing it for years." ☙

KEY TAKEAWAYS   ⊶

1. To operationalize empathy and foster a sense of internalized purpose, managers must help employees sense their impact and relationship to team and company objectives.

2. There are three essentials for integrating purpose throughout the workplace, remembered best by the acronym AIM: articulate, implement, and measure purpose.

3. ARTICULATE, STEP 1: Create a "Rallying WHY"
    a. Define the impact objective at the organization and team level. Primary tool: SASSY visions, missions and values statements

4. ARTICULATE, STEP 2: Make Culture Explicit
    a. Align execution by defining HOW the WHY is to be achieved. Primary tool: culture decks

5. IMPLEMENT, STEP 3: Specify Individual Accountabilities
    a. Ensure everyone understands how their role fits in the whole.
    b. Primary tool: ARC (Accountabilities/Resources/Consequences) agreements

6. IMPLEMENT, STEP 4: Provide Impact Feedback Loops.
    a. Help employees feel their own impact in a timely manner.
    b. Primary tools: Personal Dashboards, Peer Recognition

7. MEASURE, STEP 5: Track Leadership Effectiveness.
    a. Provide metrics and development support for managers.
    b. Primary tool: Leadership Competency Models

8. MEASURE, STEP 6: Monitor Implementation Consistency
    a. Track compliance and effectiveness of all the above people managers accountable for their people results. Primary tool: Pulse Surveys

CHAPTER 9

WHY's Golden Future

"Happiness inspires productivity."

Shawn Achor

A COMMON COMPLAINT ABOUT BUSINESS BOOKS is their one-sidedness. They often recommend new approaches and practices without considering counterarguments and other factors in play.

This chapter aims to do that.

What impact might a renewed sense of WHY at work have in coming years? Are we heading for a true Golden Age of Purpose?

We've traced the story of purpose from the origins of the species to now. We've learned why we naturally care about it and how the feeling has been dulled. We've explored why leaders should be keen to get it back, and we proposed an approach.

Less consideration has been given to trends coming down the pike. Millennials' and Gen Z's progress into management. The future of flex work. AI's maturation from amusing experiment to standard tool. All these and more open up new frontiers, possibilities, and concerns.

We're not futurists: It's beyond our intention or ability to make predictions. What we do recognize is that not all leaders are or will be convinced that a purpose program can drive engagement and help fix productivity. The way these trends play out may convince them to decide whether WHY proves to be an early-century fad, a central part of how we work, or something in between.

THE PRODUCTIVITY PUZZLE

During the dot-com boom, bullish analysts fell over one another with predictions for the internet-crazed market.

Perhaps the boldest came from Seligman Advisors' chief investment strategist. After the Dow passed the 10,000 mark in 1999, Charles Kaldec predicted it would hit 100,000 in two decades.

In fact, the index would grow by barely a fifth of that amount, ending 2020 at 30,606. For many, however, this only showed that the twenty-first century had barely tapped its potential.

Kaldec priced for perfection. He assumed the global economy would continue along the course charted by the twentieth century's close. Just as the Cold War's end had produced a peace dividend, so would the spread of democracy and capitalism deliver better conditions everywhere. Rich countries would export jobs and create new ones. Poorer nations would grow richer and create new consumers.

Like any raging bull, Kaldec was less concerned about speed bumps. From the war on terror to the financial crisis to the pandemic, unforeseen events would knock two-thirds off his estimate.

It's harder to fault him on the other third. It did not seem crazy to suppose that the 2.5 percent productivity growth the US boasted in the late '90s had a ways to go; no less than Federal Reserve Chair Alan Greenspan marveled at its staying power.

Even as he did so, however, the party was coming to an end. The measure averaged only 1.7 percent over the next two decades.

Toward the end of that dismal run, McKinsey helpfully summarized economists' diagnoses of the enduring "productivity puzzle." Causes identified range from a failure to adopt and make use of new information technologies, to creating full-time jobs where part-time was warranted, to falling demand as a result of wealth concentration and offshoring, and more (Exhibit 9.1).

The list of prognoses and solutions, alas, is much shorter. Policy-makers basically have three levers to pull—tax incentives, retraining programs, and anticompetitive action.

Relatively little thought tends to be given to what businesses might do of their own accord. Do they lack the skill to improve productivity without policy incentives—or will?

Contribution to the decline in productivity growth in France, Germany, Sweden, UK, and US from 2010–14 vs 2000–04,[1] percentage points (simple average across countries)

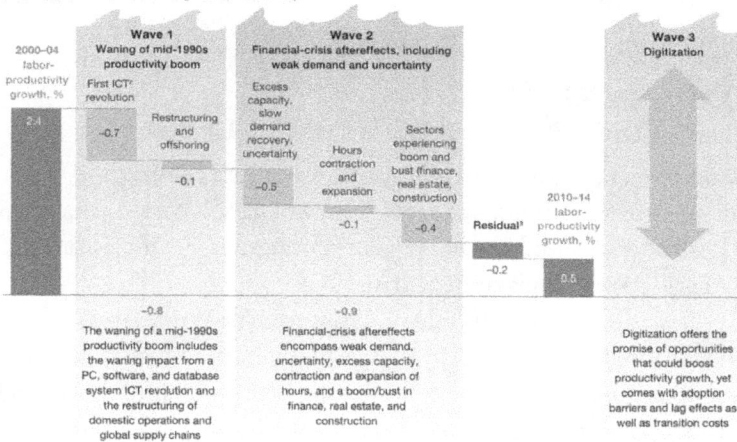

	Wave 1 Waning of mid-1990s productivity boom	Wave 2 Financial-crisis aftereffects, including weak demand and uncertainty	Wave 3 Digitization

Exhibit 9.1: Contributions to declining productivity growth in select countries, 2000–2014.

Source: McKinsey

The shareholder value prize appears to be great. A 2017 Gallup study found companies with top quartile engagement to be 21 percent more profitable than average. If all leveled up, and the Dow maintained its 7.3 percent annual growth since 2000, a "purpose-driven economy" could see not only Dow 100,000 by 2044, but 180,000.

There's good reason to temper such optimism. Between an unpredictable European land war, an increasingly assertive China, and growing protectionism and isolationism in the world's largest economy, the outlook is fraught with risk. Even the prospects for an AI-driven boom—another Roaring Twenties, as The *Economist* anticipated in 2019—are mixed. While many jobs should become more productive, countless others will be lost. "Offshoring might look like a rounding error by comparison," one Wall Street analyst has commented.

For simplicity's sake, we'll follow economists' practice of holding extraneous factors constant and focus simply on purpose at work. What share of that gleaming productivity prize might it bring about, and what might get in the way?

COUNTERPOINT: PURPOSE-FREE PRODUCTIVITY

As we've seen, making purpose work is not just challenging; failure can make teams even less engaged than when they started (chapter 8).

What if we didn't even try? Can productivity be increased without caring about engagement at all?

Consider the curious tale of Crossover for Work, an IT consultancy that bills itself as a leader in "the remote work revolution." Crossover doesn't just tolerate flexibility among its thousands of consultants; it insists upon it.

It's also an enigma: a multibillion-dollar global operation with one office, no employees, and no sales force.

To the "top 1 percent of talent" it targets, the company's pitch can sound utopian. Above-market pay. Challenging work. Unbeatable work-life balance. Yet the few who manage to land an offer—the odds are several thousand to one—quickly discover why Forbes calls Crossover "a global software sweatshop," whose contrarian management approach has made its reclusive founder one of the world's richest people.

What's going on? For starters, Crossover isn't a typical consultancy. Its "clients" are legacy software firms acquired by a sister company, with a view to streamlining and offshoring as many functions as possible. Its people are contractors, paid in ten-minute increments tracked by spyware. This amounts to a breathtakingly bold productivity play. Recall that white-collar workers seem to be on task less than three hours a day (chapter 1). By paying only for time at your desk, Crossover is effectively seeking to triple productivity. Its model is not built around roles, but standardized work streams called "pipelines." Any contractor can take over another's "pipeline" at any time. Personal relationships are all but impossible: You never meet your peers, and even direction from above is mostly through chat and email.

All this is the vision of founder Joe Liemandt. During a summer internship in the '80s, Liemandt was shocked to see how much more time his software company spent on management than programming. His solution? Kill traditional management. Forget culture and purpose. Toss out even the virtual water cooler. Instead create an "anti-company" where there's no need to care about why people are working, or about how much they believe in the value of their output. The know-how Ronald Coase saw as defining a firm (chapter 5) builds up not in workers' heads, but in a database. Engagement, if you can call it that, is driven by fear of termination.

Accordingly, the firm's Glassdoor employer reviews include tales of Dickensian suffering. Hires soon discover twelve-hour days are required to deliver the required, productive eight, making that "above market" pay, well, below market. With a deep pool of candidates who don't realize what they're signing up for, there's no shortage of bodies to step in.

Is this just an eccentric experiment, or the way of the future? Can a model that seeks not simply to ignore our need for WHY, but to actively suppress it, work in other industries? Can it be sustained?

WHAT KIND OF WORK REQUIRES WHY?

For some leaders, exhausted by years of investing in purpose with little or no return, Liemandt's path may be tempting. As the pandemic wound down, one manager told a CNBC interviewer that he "longed for the days when I didn't have to serve popcorn, and people were just grateful to have a job."

Forget costly carrots, in other words. Go all in on the stick.

The fact that few want to manage, let alone work in such an environment is telling. As societies grow rich and expand choice, they tend to reject dehumanizing practices for the simple reason that most, according to Adam Smith, find others' suffering abhorrent.

For present purposes, let's imagine a slightly less miserable version of Crossover's prototype, one that, say, demands fewer hours and allows for vacations. Could this work?

In *A Whole New Mind: Why Right-brainers Will Rule the Future*, Daniel Pink distinguished between two kinds of work based on the type of problem-solving and output required.

Algorithmic work involves a set of rules or instructions that must be followed strictly to produce the desired result. It is routine, repetitive, well-defined, and thus automatable. This does not mean "easy"—examples include manufacturing and accounting. Critically, outputs are identical no matter who does the work. Applying the correct tax rules to a company's financials should yield only one correct calculation of tax payable, for example. Standards ensure that every iPhone rolling off the line is identical to the rest. Heuristic work involves problem-solving that's more exploratory and creative, with less-defined outputs.* Examples include graphic design, marketing, and customer support, where different solutions may be considered to be of acceptable quality.

Heuristic workers follow best practices, but not comprehensive, mandatory procedures. Rather, they seek patterns, connections, and solutions that are not obvious, custom, and often novel. Such work involves cognitive empathy and an imaginative capability that must juggle many variables. For example: Do tech customers want more robust hardware or more elegant design? Are wearables helpful or intrusive? And so on.

Crossover's secret is to make its work as algorithmic as possible; its people must be smart but compliant. Algorithmic workers respond best to direct financial incentives, less to other considerations such

---

* "Heuristic" means someone discovering or learning something for themselves.

as purpose. Because every work unit is more or less identical, they cannot increase their sense of impact by putting more effort and innovation into a given unit. They can only excel by producing more units. Indeed, outstanding quality upsets the model because it raises expectations downstream.

Heuristic work is less likely to respond to such "direct-drive" incentives. Once assured of acceptable minimum compensation, what matters most to the heuristic worker is impact on internal and external customers through better deliverables. This is where the "Motivation 2.0" drivers from Pink's *Drive* come into play: Autonomy, Mastery, and Purpose (chapter 2). WHY cannot be separated from such work, and Crossover's model couldn't handle it.

A key question for leaders and managers is, thus, whether the work they're managing is more algorithmic or heuristic. Most workplaces involve some degree of both, making this a case-by-case determination: Pay a bonus to the night shift based on output and product managers for advancing the mission.

Even so, it's helpful to take note of a macrotrend shifting the entire landscape. A 2019 Brookings Institution report concluded that 25 percent of US jobs are sufficiently algorithmic to be replaced by machines in coming decades. Goldman Sachs's more recent research on AI's impact arrived at the same number. Different industries have different mixes: Brookings sees manufacturing as 90 percent automatable, for example, and white-collar management less than 15 percent automatable.

In short, we're now living in two different economies: a smaller, shrinking algorithmic one where workers respond primarily to monetary incentives and an ascendant heuristic one where more complex considerations are required.

WHAT WILL WHY WORK LOOK LIKE?

In the depths of the Great Depression, economist John Maynard Keynes published *The General Theory of Employment, Interest, and Money*, a landmark approach to fighting unemployment that policymakers embraced for almost half a century.

The Roaring Twenties found Keynes in a more optimistic frame of mind. His 1928 essay, *Economic Possibilities for Our Grandchildren*, sought to map the implications of booming productivity growth. A point would come, he believed, when societies' needs could be satisfied with far less than a forty-hour workweek, as auto manufacturer Henry Ford had recently proposed. Rather than accumulate wealth we had no time to enjoy or tolerate unemployment among those deemed surplus to an economy's requirements, we would choose to work less. Within a century, Keynes estimated, industrialized economies would embrace a fifteen-hour workweek.

What he did not foresee was a decline in productivity growth lasting nearly three-quarters of a century, where wage earners would still not reap their share of the benefits (Exhibit 9.2) or that companies would cling to the idea that at least 80 percent of jobs required forty-hour weeks.

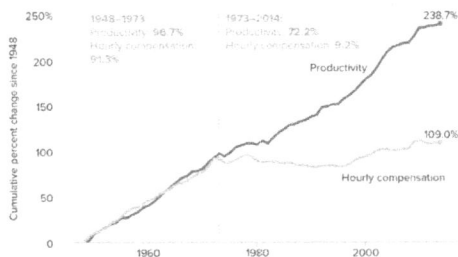

Disconnect between productivity and a typical worker's compensation, 1948–2014

Exhibit: 9.2 Productivity vs. real wages, 1948-2014.
Source: Economic Policy Institute

Today most of the workforce is technically on duty thirty-five to forty hours a week (Exhibit 9.3), but it actually works much less, perhaps as little as fifteen hours, which would prove Keynes's point.

Not only are excessive hours a drag on productivity, as McKinsey argues (Exhibit 9.1), they also alienate us from work. Anthropologist David Graeber wrote a whole book complaining about "bullshit jobs":

paid employment… so completely pointless, unnecessary, or pernicious that even the employee cannot justify its existence even though… the employee feels obliged to pretend that this is not the case.

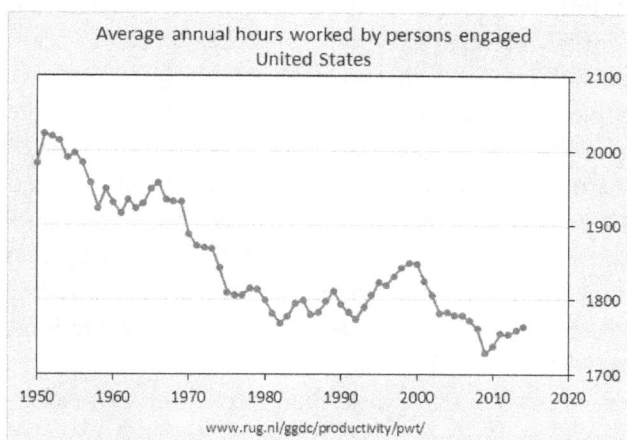

Exhibit 9.3: Average annual hours worked by persons engaged in the United States
Source: Wikipedia, Penn World Tables

Are we missing something here? Is there something about the nature of heuristic work that requires a certain amount of downtime to be productive? If so, how much? What might be the consequences of greater engagement, driven by the kind of program described in chapter 8?

Our frontline experience confirms the idea that twenty-first-century managers have got pretty good at growing productivity in algorithmic jobs; the real challenge revolves around the "heuristic 75 percent" identified by Brookings and Goldman. They may require work away from one's desk or formal meetings that Crossover's spyware would deem invalid. A business analyst, for example, may not be able to produce deliverables without time to rest their brains and engage in other activities that fuel problem-solving, including team building and other information gathering. Innovation requires trial and error, speculation, and inspiration that cannot be scheduled or forced. A growing number of workspaces, like Steve Jobs's Pixar Campus, have been designed to drive random encounters and inspire creativity—an example we discovered, fittingly, through a random podcast recommendation.

How much more can we expect of heuristic workers without fear of overwork? More than one might think. Leading and working with start-ups, we've noticed what many have remarked: Employees tend to be happier and more productive than their corporate counterparts. Many generate outsize, quality output at astonishing speed, just to reach the next milestone. We've seen large companies succeed in replicating such cultures, typically on a team-by-team basis, driven by inspiring, attentive management. Generally, however, productivity expectations in corporate environments remain shockingly low, even though there's no proven morale benefit to low expectations. More often, there's a measurable cost.

We've seen the tactics described in chapter 8 transform average or sluggish teams. There is no need to demand, like Crossover, optimal efficiency all the time, like a vehicle cruising on a highway. Most roles have more in common with the stops and starts of city driving. Still, there appears to be significant upside that can be realized without coming close to interfering with thinking, learning, and team building.

Where does that leave the "algorithmic 25 percent" when it comes to purpose? Should their managers tack away from engagement as a distraction, focusing instead on better aligning pay with output?

Research suggests not. Sweatshops are not just hellish, but demonstrably inefficient. A Better Work study of 1,300 Vietnamese garment factories suggests profitability increases with humane working conditions. The persistence of sweatshops has more to do with "deficient managerial capital" with a lack of motivational know-how rivaling that of the Industrial Revolution (chapter 2).

Crossover's model may work in its sector since legacy software maintenance is about squeezing value out of old products, not creating new ones. Arguably, it also involves deceptive hiring and compensation practices, mind-numbing work, unsustainable productivity targets, and unsustainable talent churn. With work units narrowly constrained and workers deliberately isolated, the firm cannot accumulate more than rudimentary knowledge applicable to a limited problem set. It does not seem replicable to handle a quarter of the economy, which may not be in human hands much longer (the model may well work powered by AI).

WHY + AI = ?

Let's look at AI head on. As noted earlier in this chapter, algorithmic roles are perfect for machines and bots. Fewer are going to find themselves doing such work. The economy will become ever more heuristic.

If the history of innovation is anything to go by, as AI eliminates and reduces roles, it will make the rest more productive. Goldman Sachs believes generative AI could grow productivity by 1.5 percent a year by the 2030s, with a 7 percent cumulative rise in global GDP.

But what, exactly, are we applying AI to? Some productivity technologies make existing practices more efficient, much as the Cloud did for certain forms of collaboration. They can also enable practices that were not viable or even imaginable before, like the use of social media in marketing.

We see potential for AI to have a material impact on the program described in chapter 8, making several of the steps easier and more valuable.

The greatest barrier to constructing meaningful employee feedback loops cited by our clients is the investment of time and money required to gather and process personal and team impact data in a timely manner. As in any situation where data is hard to come by, managers look for low-hanging proxies, in this case, available metrics like task completion rates and peer recognition. These go a long way.

But what if the process could be made more efficient and comprehensive, for instance, if AI could tap virtually all data generated by individual and team activities, quickly turning these into meaningful and motivating metrics? Given the powerful, rapidly growing capabilities of current beta products, we believe such a leap forward, in the form of an AI-driven dashboard sector, could be eminently achievable in the next decade.

When this happens, today's ingenious workarounds may be replaced. The economic viability of such practices will stretch to many more companies. Millions of workers will gain a new sense of impact. AI may not only push us toward a purpose economy by cutting algorithmic jobs, it might pull us there.

WILL MANAGERS PLAY BALL?

We've started talking about the future of WHY from leaders' and companies' perspective. From the ground we covered in chapters 2 and 3, we must not lose sight of the psychological needs and predispositions of the people upon whose behavior companies are dependent (as we saw in chapter 8): the managers. Many business books, including this one, effectively assume frontline managers will be willing and able to support the change senior leaders want to see. Is that fair?

Consider the journey of entrepreneur Dov Siedman's 2011 book, *How: Why How We Do Anything Means Everything.* Building upon a 2004 article making "the case for ethical leadership," it carried the weight of great expectations, attracting praise from Tony Robbins and Arianna Huffington and nabbing a foreword by former President Bill Clinton plus an invitation to speak to the UN General Assembly.

The problem Siedman sought to address was the "unethical leadership" he saw as the root cause of the young century's spectacular business failures, from the collapse of Enron to the global financial crisis. His solution? Ethical leadership. This would drive business performance by increasing trust, collaboration, and problem-solving, while reducing compliance and legal distractions. Performance was not just about getting things done, Siedman wrote:

> *[It was also about] getting the right things done in the right way, at the right time, for the right reasons…to create value for ourselves, our organizations, and society as a whole.*

As compelling as many found the argument, however, the book never achieved the kind of transformative impact supporters expected. After a respectable 18-week run on the *New York Times* bestseller list, it fell in search popularity and left the stage.

The work's admirable intentions appear to have been undone by a circularity in its premise. Seidman assumed as his solution the phenomenon that defined his problem: the ability of unethical leaders to see that ethical leadership is in their best interest. It wasn't that the perpetrators of these scandals didn't know the case for acting honestly; they just didn't buy it. As a C-suite leader who still had a copy of *How* in her office a decade later observed, "The solution to bad behavior can't just be a call for good behavior."

This kind of argument is far from unfamiliar in business and self-help books. As we saw in chapter 2, the most popular approach to finding our WHY starts with the assumption that we already possess a singular, lifelong purpose that we can articulate and must live by—without considering the possibility that maybe we don't, can't, and shouldn't.

If there's a place where this book's program might get in trouble, it would be to assume that managers will naturally grasp and fall in line with a call to operationalize empathy by providing better purpose, cultural clarity, and support/feedback mechanisms to their teams.

Great managers are in rare supply, we know. Out of every five American workers, four blame workplace misery on their direct supervisor. and three say they're more likely to trust a total stranger.

So where are those we need to come from?

We believe the potential to grow better managers is far greater than these last numbers suggest. Yes, sociopaths tend to be overrepresented in management ranks, estimated to account for up to 20 percent versus 5 percent in the general population. That still leaves a well-meaning, cooperative majority. Roughly 10 percent of workers have the "inherent ability to manage," according to Gallup. This may not be enough for larger companies, which can require up to twice as many, but it's a start.

This shifts the challenge of change away from frontline managers themselves to higher-ups. Their imperative is not simply to "better", but to take managing managers more seriously, from selection and training to feedback and development support.

Gallup estimates 82 percent of managers are either unqualified, temperamentally unsuited, or disinterested in the role, preferring advisory or what Shopify calls "crafter" roles, focused on direct product work. Managers themselves are all too aware of their shortcomings. Fifty-eight percent claim to have received no training. A quarter feel weak at conflict resolution, and almost as many struggle to motivate their teams. One in six feels lost in supporting performance improvement and career development—both critical engagement drivers, as we saw in chapter 3.

In this light, is it any wonder their teams' engagement remains so low?

The solution cannot be for millions of managers to pick up books like this one (though we wouldn't object) and act on the insights. If we simply exhort managers to "get the right things done in the right way at the right time for the right reasons," we'll be, like Siedman, Sinek, and others, assuming our solution as a precondition. We can do better.

BUILD, MEASURE, LEARN

"What gets measured, gets improved." That idea, often attributed to Peter Drucker, seems to be manifested in many aspects of life, from skill development to physical health. Less obvious is *how* to measure the right things. Someone looking to get in shape by only measuring weight, as opposed to body fat or waist size, could fall prey to a harmful crash diet.

As we saw with Bruce Henderson's Story of Joe (chapter 8), measuring managers by the wrong yardstick can have dire consequences. If shareholders desire long-term profit growth but managers' performance is assessed based on short-term metrics like profitability, neither may get what they want. It's encouraging to see companies move from pure financial metrics to human capital (HC) ones, which emphasize investment in people. For many, however, there's clearly a ways to go.

We've found experiences like those of the software company in chapter 8, whose diversity goals were undermined by a toxic division head, to be far from rare. Great companies generally have great business units led by great managers. But they can also have terrible ones, led by individuals whose divergent agendas are masked or excused by good numbers.

Driving purpose through an organization must start above the heads of frontline and divisional managers, at the level of senior leadership teams and even boards. Those that truly care about long-term value creation—that is, anyone without an exit or wind-up planned—must insist on seeing human capital indicators as well as financial ones, and they must evaluate CEO or managerial performance in this light.

Taking purpose seriously at the CEO or board level means asking leadership to:

- Establish an HC dashboard for the entire organization that also breaks out at the divisional team level, featuring employee engagement levels and leadership development scores as well as team-by-team turnover and retention.
- Take frequent pulse surveys and conduct occasional deep dives into engagement-related and Q12 subjects.
- Collect feedback via anonymous, virtual suggestion boxes that also functions as a whistle-blowing channel (a best practice in any event).
- Dive into the causes and solutions when employees flag inconsistencies between the company's goals and practices.

- Hire and promote managers based not on their ability to interview well and manage upward but to drive engagement and alignment.
- Set divisional and team targets and hold managers accountable for shortfalls, plus consider even having these measures be a part of the bonus compensation plans.
- Have a zero-tolerance policy on toxic behavior at all levels, even if they are delivering their numbers.
- Accept above-average turnover in management positions as a reasonable price for preventing even greater disruption among employees generally.
- Support managers with policies and HR/HC structures that support their engagement and alignment efforts. (No individual manager can make up for reorganizations that leave remaining employees overwhelmed or for incentive programs that incentivize other behaviors.) Make engagement everyone's goal and problem, including the CFO's and COO's.

For all this to work, leaders and managers don't need to be particularly well meaning: just duly governed, which companies in Fortune's Best Places to Work lists, for example, have shown to be doable even by very large organizations. Breaking down and capturing the right metrics turns the desire to earn and advance into a focus on the Magic Three value drivers: fit, alignment, and engagement (chapter 5).

What leaders do require, and what these great companies demonstrate daily, is the ability to see things from their reports' and stakeholders' perspective, or cognitive empathy (chapter 7). This does not mean good intentions, per Adam Smith. Managers don't need to care for employees the way they do family and friends. They just need to recognize that employee engagement is essential, there's no way to fake it—and there are no shortcuts.

THE NEXT GENERATIONS

By 2044, millennials will be approaching retirement. The average Gen Zer will be almost forty. Together they will occupy most management and leadership roles.

As we've seen, they already have distinctive feelings about purpose and work (chapter 3). More than half report a sense of limited advancement prospects, which has left over 40 percent of them more anxious, up to 72 percent more concerned with work-life balance (versus 58 percent of baby boomers), and virtually all more keen about flexible work arrangements than previous generations.

They've felt emboldened to question how they've been managed. They tell researchers they want to see more ethical, caring, and diverse management, as well as more responsibility and transparency. Two in three care about social impact and purpose at work; less than two in five feel they get it. The sense that their workplace aspirations may be out of reach has contributed to unprecedented emotional withdrawal. "I don't think my career defines me," one millennial told Gallup. "It's just something I have to do."

Unaddressed, such sentiments do not bode well. One veteran Silicon Valley recruiter worries we could be heading for a world where "managers are more disengaged than ever…just phoning it in." On the other hand, she notes: "They may turn out to be the most empathetic managers ever."

We believe the latter possibility more likely. Trends tend to correct themselves, especially downward ones. Emerging from early career malaise through promotion, growing responsibility, and a greater financial stake in their companies' performance, these "lost" generations are likely to appreciate their reports' aspirations and frustrations better than past managers. They may well create the purpose-driven workplace they now long for.

Younger workers we've worked with in writing this book have proven to be not only the source of some of its most powerful ideas ("we need to hear ourselves play"), but also its recommendations' most enthusiastic testers. "Companies needs to stop trying to persuade us how impactful they are," begged one. "Help us feel how impactful *we* are."

At least one other millennial and Gen Z aspiration may amplify this generational desire to have and feel impact: right-sizing the place of work in our lives.

When the standard 48-hour (or six-day) week was cut to 40 hours in the 1930s and '40s, productivity and output went up (chapter 4). Economists like Juliet Shor believe the same will happen if we shortened the workweek again, even with compensation unchanged. Personal distractions at work, replaced by focus. Stress and burnout, down. Productivity and well-being, up. Mounting evidence supports this theory.*

A shorter workweek is not on the immediate horizon, nor does it promise to be a panacea for declining productivity growth or the problem of so-called bullshit jobs. In live-to-work cultures like the US, such a shift will certainly meet resistance. But for many, it may prove a powerful demonstration of leadership's commitment to productivity and well-being as two sides of the same coin, and an inspiring instance of aligning walk with talk.

Curiously, leaders who are most skeptical of remote work arrangements tend to be more open to the idea of tighter weeks.

"If we can't see and work together as a team, we're not going to learn as a team," one told us. "But if we can learn together to do five days of work in four, I'm all in."

THE WHY WE ALL SHARE

WHY's bright future—a world of invigorated employees, revitalized productivity growth, and growing wealth for the species—is hardly inevitable. Yet conditions are promising. These include:

---

* Perpetual Guardian, a New Zealand-based financial services company, found a 20 percent reduction in hours increased weekly productivity by 4 percent and engagement by 20 percent. Microsoft saw productivity increase 40 percent when it tried the same in its Japanese operations. The German supermarket chain Aldi has long been operating on a four-day workweek with sustained productivity but significantly reduced turnover.

- *Years of sustained effort* to leverage and learn from purpose;
- *New technologies* that can make personal impact tracking easier and more inspiring;
- *An AI-driven shift toward heuristic work* where purpose has its greatest productivity impact;
- *A growing sense* among leaders that the workplace is reimagining itself whether they like it or not; and
- *A rising generation of leaders and managers* that have experienced WHY done wrong and want to get it right.

All these factors, together with a better grasp on how WHY works, gives us much positive change to anticipate in the workplace. But what about in general life, as individuals? If we expect we'll only be able to feel purposeful once our bosses get their act together, we could be waiting a while. How might purpose show up differently in the meantime? How can we own our sense of WHY?

One clue lies in an observation of the award-winning documentarian Ann Druyan. "We are a story-driven species," she said. "We understand how things are put together in the context of narrative."

Human beings have been storytellers since before we began mapping the tales of great hunts on the walls of caves. Stories are not just reports of things that have happened. The ones we repeat and come back to have common elements. Disorder and risk are introduced to a stable world, in the form of mystery, threat, or opportunity. Protagonists go out of their way, often reluctantly, to restore balance. The journey is fraught with obstacles and setbacks. Eventually we get there. The end...until next time.*

Therapists often encourage clients to think of their struggles and aspirations as the seeds of their own stories. The stakes are far higher than the ones we read or watch. While challenges are guaranteed, a favorable ending is not. For some, such uncertainty is undesirable, to be resolved or avoided as swiftly as possible. For others, it is what

---

* One of the most compelling accounts of human beings' relationship with story is Joseph Campbell's 1949 classic, *The Hero With a Thousand Faces*, which reads in many ways like a history of our journey as a species—and inspired George Lucas to write *Star Wars*.

makes life worth living. Hindu mythology turns on the notion that a single divine being would find omnipotence, omniscience, and eternal life so boring that it would rather fragment itself into countless imperfect, confused, mortal creatures—all trying to understand their own journey—and here we are.

We've come to see this notion, of a high stakes story with no guarantees, as the fruitful way to think about our personal relationship with WHY.

All the elements are there. Many of us have often gone for years, even much of our lives, without thinking about purpose. Our sense of malaise and/or encounter with the question creates the challenge. Thereafter, we become heroes in our own narratives, seeking at least a working solution. We learn about ourselves and the world along the way. When we find our answer, order is restored, for a time. But our story doesn't end there. Our changing world and selves all but guarantee things will fall out of place again—and then we'll find ourselves starring in our own sequel.

Conversations we've had in the course of writing this book have drawn our attention to a related insight. Even when instability rages around a fictional protagonist, one thing stays consistent: They are still the hero, and the narrative, still a story. Likewise, as we embark on our quest and seek out situations where we can have a positive impact on others—even before we're sure we're heading in the right direction—we cannot help but have impact on another valued part of the world: us.

Mixed in with the other-oriented discoveries and insights we generate every day—the bulk of the WHY Iceberg (chapter 6)—are discoveries and insights that relate primarily to ourselves. The first category, how spotting a pattern in customer behavior might lead to a successful product, for example, typically requires time and teamwork to turn into impact. The second, expanding our knowledge, memories, and capacity for new ideas, happens right away.

Given the shortcomings of much formal education, in school and the workplace, "learning" has come to have connotations of drudgery for many. Yet as new parents and primary teachers know, we all begin life as natural learners, effortlessly deriving joy from new knowledge. Even a jaded teen doomscrolling on TikTok is feeding an impulse that started as a quest for interesting information. In adult life, our love of discovery continues to manifest itself through making new friends, discovering new shows, visiting new places, and so on.

When we own this love of discovery, we can begin to learn from it. We can become more engaged, efficient, and effective learners. As Plato, Abraham Maslow, and scientists of well-being have argued, better understanding ourselves and the world, even without a specific objective, makes us happier (chapter 6). We can appreciate our own journey, even, if not especially, in its darker moments, as a story that gets its value not simply through discoveries and victories, but mysteries and setbacks.

The feeling of simply enjoying and gaining from the search for personal impact: This is the WHY we all share. We don't need a calling or statement to experience it. It's what you did at work last week. What you will do next. What you'll do for the rest of your life. The trick is simply to be mindful: as researcher Jon Kabat-Zinn puts it, to "pay attention, on purpose, in the present moment, nonjudgmentally."

No matter how we approach it, our WHY, personal or collective, will often feel mysterious. The idea of WHY itself should not. Purpose is not a mystical force. It's not something we're born with, nor a teenage dream by which we must constrain our lives, nor something we can discover, once and for all, by talking it out.

Purpose, like love or fairness, is a feeling generated by thoughts. The need for and experience of it has helped humanity rise from a cluster of vulnerable individuals an alien visitor might have deemed destined for extinction, to the most collaborative, adaptive, and thriving species in the universe. Every day it inspires us to do better by our planet and each other—and if we don't have it, to search for it.

The search is not to be undervalued. By the order of things, we spend more of our lives searching than finding.

WHY is less something we have than something we live.

It's a journey. A story. Even... a kind of verb.

And you're doing it right now. ⟳

KEY TAKEAWAYS   ⌒━

1. In the near future, business purpose will need to interact with at least three significant changes in order to be effective:
   a. Millennials and Gen Zers' progression to management
   b. The endurance of remote and hybrid work
   c. The rise of generative artificial intelligence (AI)
2. Policy changes and technological advances may solve pieces of our productivity puzzle, but little progress will be made toward growth without addressing the core problem of employee engagement.
3. WHY-weary managers will be tempted to emulate models like that of the purposeless consultancy Crossover, but this won't work for most of the economy.
4. WHY's ability to add value to the current workplace landscape depends on the shifting line between algorithmic jobs and heuristic ones—currently at a 25 percent to 75 percent split, respectively.
5. With AI taking over algorithmic work, we're heading toward an economy that is largely heuristic and requires purpose implementations to drive productivity.
6. The rise in AI productivity, combined with Gen Z and millennial managers' demands for work-life balance, may push businesses to embrace shorter workweeks, potentially unlocking greater output than the century-old, forty-hour standard.
7. It is critical for boards and executive leadership to take engagement measures seriously or disengagement will continue to drag productivity.
8. Top-down implementation will also help tackle the problem of inconsistency between the management's words and their actions—often a mismatch that erodes trust, feeds cynicism, and kills engagement.
9. Regardless of where the company, managers, or fellow employees are on the quest for WHY-driven productivity and happiness, we can live out our individual, ever-changing WHYs by focusing on our journey. We need to keep top of mind that we are always impacting ourselves through learning.

10. This perpetual discovery is the WHY we all share—not a mystical force to leverage but a journey to enjoy...and an action, a verb we do every day.

AFTERWORD

Next Steps

"Enjoy your problems."

D.T. Suzuki

The problem of purpose at work is not new. In fact, as this book conveys, it's been with us so long it can seem insoluble. Which reminds me of a Zen story:

An unhappy young man calls on a wise old master high up in the mountains.

"Why are you here?" the master asks, answering the door.

"To relieve my suffering," replies the man.

"I'm busy," says the master, retreating inside. "Wait there."

A few days later, the master opens his door, surprised to see the young man there shivering in the snow.

"You! Why are you here again?" asks the master.

"To relieve my suffering," says the man.

The master laughs: "Then get out of the snow!"

As managers and employees, we are often so caught up in our challenges that we miss the ways our thoughts have become the problem. We get stuck. We think we've done our part and wait for others to do the rest.

We need to get out of the snow.

This is especially true when it comes to purpose. With something that feels at once so important and perplexing, the temptation to let a guru solve the problem for us is strong.

Thankfully, the authors' intention in *Why Is a Verb* has not been to provide The Answer, so much as to model an approach.

The best way to make their effort is to move forward with the same mix of curiosity, critical thinking, and pragmatism that has characterized these pages.

So don't just read.

Question. Try. Reflect.

Note what works for you, what doesn't, and learn from the differences.

Share your discoveries.

Above all, enjoy the process.

For this is the path to living your WHY.

Jen Sanning
Vice President and Executive Partner
Forrester Research, Inc.
Denver, February 2024

Acknowledgments

An unrepayable debt is owed to clients of BDC's Growth Driver Program who first brought the problem of business purpose to my attention—they know who they are—and the leaders, friends, and Framework clients who gave me the confidence to believe I could help solve it. Of particular note are those who took time to comment as the solution evolved from a half-day workshop about making missions matter into a comprehensive, co-authored book. These include but are not limited to: Philippe Achkar, Mark Benning, Tania Corbett, Bill Ciprick, Renée Colyer, Pierre Doyon, David Flueck, Jason Green, Keith Halliday, Stephen Harper, Eric Hillmer, Lisa Hyde, Peter LePiane, Patricia Phillips, Mark Sampson, Tom Short, Brian Singh, Chris Thrall, Bryce Tingle, and Richard Turski. Thank you all.

I am grateful to spirited skeptics from Marcus Aurelius to Zanny Minton Beddoes, whose courage, lucidity and wit have long inspired me with the power of the pen; to my Cambridge teachers, John Dunn, Istvan Hont, and Michael Sonenscher, who showed me how to wield one; and to BCG mentors like Mari-Ellen Murray and David Pecaut, who taught me how to get to the point.

Further thanks are due to the 2023 TEDx University of Alberta committee for helping me squeeze much of this argument into a sixteen-minute talk, to TEDx for featuring it to its global subscribers, and to the tens of thousands whose views, likes and comments gave this expanded version a tailwind as we approached launch.

Above all, I must thank my wife, Stacy Stewart, for her guidance, faith and partnership as we progress between WHYs together; to our families for their support and understanding; and of course, the insightful, pragmatic, and visionary Karissa Price, without whom this would be less than half of what it is. —SB

As with many achievements in life, there are many people whose support and assistance have truly made it possible and to whom I owe so much gratitude. First and foremost, I'd like to thank my coauthor and friend, Stephen Butler, who reached out two years ago and asked if I'd like to join him on this adventure. Thank you, Stephen, for the mental stimulation, camaraderie, and dedication to bringing this book to life!

Secondly, of course, is my family without whom life would not be as purposeful. To my life partner and husband, Juan Rico, and my son, Santiago Rico, thank you for your daily love and opportunities to learn and grow as a person.

To the many friends and colleagues who've offered direct support, input, ideas, suggestions, experiences—Dan Witters, Patrick Bogart, Jennifer Sanning, Sophia Yen, Jenny Illum, Stephen Lytle, Jessica Jensen, Martina Bradford, LeeAnne Linderman, Tracey Brown,- Toby Arnett, Summer Baldwin, Cynthia Nelson, Jackie Hernandez, Carla Giovannetti Dodds, Diana Dass, Diana Jones, James Johnson, Rodney Niya, Karthik Parameswaran, John Briggs, Laura Pinkett, Lara Small, Tom VanGilder, Andrea Albright, to name a few—many thanks.

To the leaders who've stood out in my career as truly exceptional in creating an opportunity to live my purpose and feel my impact, a huge thank you to Sean Slovenksi, Valeria Rico, Charles Redfield, Latriece Watkins, and Sandy McCullough.

And last but not least, a debt of gratitude goes to Sam Walton who created a system of values and culture at Walmart that lives on long after him and truly inspires many people to live their best lives in service of helping families save money so they can live better. —KP

The authors would also like to thank Ty Breland and Jennifer Sanning for their invaluable contributions; Carol Reed, Nathaniel Roy, Carmen Smith, Lisa Stumpf and Simon Yates for their editorial and design expertise; Eric Jorgensen, Emmy Koziak, and the team at Scribe for publication support; and all our endorsers for their early readership and support.

Sources By Chapter

Note: Sources used more than once are cited once, in the earliest chapter in which they appear.

Preface: Making WHY Work

Adkins, B. A. (2023, March 31). *What Millennials Want From Work and Life*. Gallup.com. https://www.gallup.com/workplace/236477/millennials-work-life.aspx.

Beinhocker, E. D. (2006). *The Origin of Wealth: Evolution, Complexity, and the Radical Remaking of Economics*. Harvard Business Press.

Business Roundtable Redefines the Purpose of a Corporation to Promote 'An Economy That Serves All Americans.'(n.d.). Business Roundtable. https://www.businessroundtable.org/business-roundtable-redefines-the-purpose-of-a-corporation-to-promote-an-economy-that-serves-all-americans.

Customer Service Representatives : Occupational Outlook Handbook: U.S. Bureau of Labor Statistics. (2022, September 8). https://www.bls.gov/ooh/office-and-administrative-support/customer-service-representatives.htm.

Drucker, P. F. (1974). *Management: Tasks, Responsibilities, Practices*. New York : Harper & Row.

Gallup, Inc. (2023). *State of the Global Workplace Report*—Gallup. In Gallup.com. https://www.gallup.com/workplace/349484/state-of-the-global-workplace.aspx.

Gallup, Inc. (2023a, April 3). *Gallup's Q12 Employee Engagement Survey*—Gallup. Gallup.com. https://www.gallup.com/workplace/356063/gallup-q12-employee-engagement-survey.aspx.

Google Search Statistics—Internet Live Stats. (n.d.). https://www.internetlivestats.com/google-search-statistics/.

Google Trends. (n.d.). Trends. Purpose, WHY, all dates. https://trends.google.com/trends/explore?hl=en-GB&tz=360&date=all&hl=en-GB&q=Purpose,WHY&sni=3.

Harari, Y. N. (2014). *Sapiens: A Brief History of Humankind.* Random House.

Hastwell, C. (n.d.). *Top 5 Things Millennials Want In the Workplace in 2021. Great Place to Work.* https://www.greatplacetowork.com/resources/blog/top-5-things-millennials-want-in-the-workplace-in-2021-as-told-by-millennials.

Hidaka, B. H. (2012). *Depression as a disease of modernity: Explanations for increasing prevalence. Journal of Affective Disorders,* 140(3), 205–214. https://doi.org/10.1016/j.jad.2011.12.036.

Income Tax: Business Purpose, Tax Avoidance, and Section 355 on JSTOR. (n.d.). https://www.jstor.org/stable/3479320.

Kelly, J. (2023, March 31). "Goldman Sachs Predicts 300 Million Jobs Will Be Lost or Degraded by Artificial Intelligence." Forbes. https://www.forbes.com/sites/jackkelly/2023/03/31/goldman-sachs-predicts-300-million-jobs-will-be-lost-or-degraded-by-artificial-intelligence/?sh=4a6efdcf782b.

Lloyd, V. (2022, February 11). "What gets measured gets improved." *theHRDIRECTOR.* https://www.thehrdirector.com/features/big-data/what-gets-measured-gets-improved/#:~:text=This%20was%20recognised%20by%20the,it%20all%20to%20inform%20decisions.

Mautz, S. (2021, January 5). "A 27-Year Study Says 1 Thing Is Key to Happiness and Longevity in Work and Life." Inc.com. https://www.inc.com/scott-mautz/a-27-year-study-says-1-thing-is-key-to-happiness-longevity-in-work-life.html.

McKinsey & Company, *Solving the productivity puzzle.* (2018, February 20). McKinsey & Company. https://www.mckinsey.com/featured-insights/regions-in-focus/solving-the-productivity-puzzle.

O'Donnell, J. (2021, January 5). "Are You a Toxic Boss? Google's Management Study Will Tell You. Inc.com." https://www.inc.com/jt-odonnell/googles-detailed-management-study-reveals-8-signs-youre-a-toxic-boss.html.

Pink, D. H. (2009). *Drive: The Surprising Truth About What Motivates Us.* National Geographic Books.

Schwantes, M. (n.d.). "The No. 1 Reason Why Employees Quit Their Managers." www.linkedin.com. https://www.linkedin.com/pulse/1-reason-why-employees-quit-managers-marcel-schwantes/.

Sheth, R. (2023). "75 Must-Know Customer Experience Statistics to Move Your Business Forward." SmartKarrot L Comprehensive Customer Success. https://www.smartkarrot.com/resources/blog/customer-experience-statistics/#:~:text=89%25%20of%20businesses%20compete%20primarily,warm%20and%20friendly%20customer%20experience.

Sinek, S., Mead, D., & Docker, P. (2017). *Find Your Why*: A Practical Guide for Discovering Purpose for You and Your Team. Penguin UK.

Stengel, J. Why Purpose : *Jim Stengel.* (n.d.). https://www.jimstengel.com/purpose/.

Sorkin, A. R. (2019, January 17). "World's Biggest Investor Tells C.E.O.s Purpose Is the 'Animating Force' for Profits." *The New York Times.* https://www.nytimes.com/2019/01/17/business/dealbook/blackrock-larry-fink-letter.html.

Sound Business Purpose. (n.d.). Google Books. https://books.google.ca/books/about/Sound_Business_Purpose.html?id=BdoPAQAAMAA-J&redir_esc=y.

"The Productivity–Pay Gap." (n.d.). Economic Policy Institute. https://www.epi.org/productivity-pay-gap/#:~:text=From%201979%20to%202020%2C%20net,(after%20adjusting%20for%20inflation).

Thorpe, D. (2018, February 23). We Are In "The Golden Age of Purpose" so How Do We Capitalize on It? *Forbes.* https://www.forbes.com/sites/devinthorpe/2018/02/23/we-are-in-the-golden-age-of-purpose-so-how-do-we-capitalize-on-it/?sh=463124aa5f13.

Vouchercloud (n.d.-b). "How Many Productive Hours in a Work Day? Just 2 Hours, 23 Minutes. . .Vouchercloud." https://www.vouchercloud.com/resources/office-worker-productivity.

"Why your business needs to invest in Corporate Social Impact—Duke Corporate Education." (2018b, December 3). Duke Corporate Education. https://www.dukece.com/insights/why-your-business-needs-in-

vest-corporate-social-impact/#:~:text=Not%20your%20father%27s%20
CSR&text=In%20the%20US%2C%20Fortune%20500,the%20form%20-
of%20product%20donations.

Chapter 1: Our Purpose Paradox

"2023 Edelman Trust Barometer." (n.d.). Edelman. https://www.edelman.
com/trust/2023/trust-barometer.

"Civilian Labor Force Level." (2023, June 2). https://fred.stlouisfed.org/
series/CLF16OV.

"Civilian labor force participation rate. "(n.d.). https://www.bls.gov/charts/
employment-situation/civilian-labor-force-participation-rate.htm.

Colvin, G. (2021, August 5). "America's top CEOs didn't live up to their promises in Business Roundtable letter, researchers find." *Fortune*. https://fortune.
com/2021/08/05/business-roundtable-letter-statement-on-the-pur-
pose-of-a-corporation-stakeholder-capitalism-american-ceos/.

"Engage for Good Resources." (n.d.). https://engageforgood.com/resources/.

Friedman, M. (1970, September 13). "A Friedman doctrine—The Social
Responsibility of Business Is to Increase Its Profits." *New York Times*. https://
www.nytimes.com/1970/09/13/archives/a-friedman-doctrine-the-so-
cial-responsibility-of-business-is-to.html.

Gallup, Inc. (2013, July 23). *State of the Global Workplace 2013 | Gallup Topic*.
https://www.gallup.com/topic/state-of-the-global-workplace-2013.aspx.

Gallup, Inc. (2013b, July 23). *State of the Global Workplace 2013 | Gallup
Topic*. https://www.gallup.com/topic/state-of-the-global-workplace-2013.
aspx.

Google Search Statistics—Internet Live Stats. (n.d.). https://www.internet
livestats.com/google-search-statistics/.

Google Trends. (n.d.). Trends. Purpose, WHY, all dates. https://trends.
google.com/trends/explore?date=all&q=Purpose,WHY&hl=en-GB

Huff, S. (2022, December 17). "Marc Benioff Tells Salesforce Employees
New Hires Are Less Productive." *Entrepreneur*. https://www.entrepreneur.

com/business-news/marc-benioff-tell-salesforce-employees-in-slack-message/441343.

Hume, D. (2018). *A Treatise of Human Nature: Being an Attempt to Introduce the Experimental Method of Reasoning Into Moral Subjects.* . . . of 3; Volume 2. Gale Ecco, Print Editions.

JUST Capital. "More Than Half of the Companies in This Year's JUST 100 Are Business Roundtable Signatories—JUST Capital." (n.d.). JUST Capital. https://justcapital.com/reports/more-than-half-of-just-100-signed-business-roundtable-statement-on-stakeholder-capitalism/.

Keller, H. (1996). *The Story of My Life.* Dover Publications.

"Labor productivity rose at 1.1-percent annual rate from fourth quarter 2019 to first quarter 2023" : *The Economics Daily*: U.S. Bureau of Labor Statistics. (2023, May 17). https://www.bls.gov/opub/ted/2023/labor-productivity-rose-at-1-1-percent-annual-rate-from-fourth-quarter-2019-to-first-quarter-2023.htm.

MacDonald, B. (2016). *Anybody Can Do Anything.* HarperCollins.

McLoughlin, D. (2023, January 17). Self-Help Books Statistics. https://wordsrated.com/self-help-books-statistics/.

purpose | Search Online Etymology Dictionary. (n.d.). https://www.etymonline.com/search?q=purpose

PwC, "The Purpose Gap—Corporate reporting"—PwC UK blogs. (n.d.). https://pwc.blogs.com/corporatereporting/2020/10/the-purpose-gap-october-2020.html.

Boston College Center for Corporate Citizenship (n.d.). "State of Corporate Citizenship 2022 Infographic." BC CCC. https://ccc.bc.edu/content/ccc/digital-knowledge-products/state-of-corporate-citizenship-2022-infographic.html.

Simon, Herbert, "A Behavioral Model of Rational Choice on JSTOR." (n.d.). https://www.jstor.org/stable/1884852.

Sinek, S. (2011). *Start With Why*: The Inspiring Million-Copy Bestseller That Will Help You Find Your Purpose. Penguin.

"The Science of Stuck | Britt Frank - Listen - Do It With Dan." (n.d.). Chartable. https://chartable.com/podcasts/do-it-with-dan/episodes/111849133-the-science-of-stuck-britt-frank.

Top Executives : Occupational Outlook Handbook: U.S. Bureau of Labor Statistics. (2022, September 8). https://www.bls.gov/ooh/management/top-executives.htm.

University College London (2022, May 6). "Opinion: Is there a happiness equation? Here's how we're trying to." *UCL News.* https://www.ucl.ac.uk/news/2021/may/opinion-there-happiness-equation-heres-how-were-trying-find-out.

Watts, Alan (2022). Not What Should Be, But What Is. Alan Watts Organization. https://alanwatts.org/transcripts/not-what-should-be-but-what-is/.

Winston, A. (2021, September 17). *Is the Business Roundtable Statement Just Empty Rhetoric? Harvard Business Review.* https://hbr.org/2019/08/is-the-business-roundtable-statement-just-empty-rhetoric.

Witters, B. D. (2023, June 27). "U.S. Depression Rates Reach New Highs." Gallup.com. https://news.gallup.com/poll/505745/depression-rates-reach-new-highs.aspx.

Wittgenstein, L. (2010). *Philosophical Investigations.* John Wiley & Sons.

Chapter 2: Why Now? How We Got Here

Bain & Company (2023, February 22) *Purpose, Mission, and Vision Statements.* Bain. https://www.bain.com/insights/management-tools-mission-and-vision-statements/.

Ballard, J. (2019). "Millennials are the loneliest generation." *YouGov.* https://today.yougov.com/topics/society/articles-reports/2019/07/30/loneliness-friendship-new-friends-poll-survey.

Braun, S., Wesche, J. S., Frey, D., Weisweiler, S., & Peus, C. (2012). "Effectiveness of mission statements in organizations – A review." *Journal of Management & Organization,* 18(4), 430–444. https://doi.org/10.5172/jmo.2012.18.4.430

Collins, J., (2001). *Good to Great: Why Some Companies Make the Leap . . . and Others Don't.* Random House.

Das, S. (2023). "What Makes Something Go Viral? The Psychology of Virality." *Feedough*. https://www.feedough.com/why-things-go-viral/.

Definition of company. (2023). In *Merriam-Webster Dictionary*. https://www.merriam-webster.com/dictionary/company.

"EY, The Business Case for Purpose" (2016, April 24). *Harvard Business Review*. https://hbr.org/sponsored/2016/04/the-business-case-for-purpose.

Godin, S. (2018). *This Is Marketing: You Can't Be Seen Until You Learn to See*. Penguin.

Goleman, D. (2006). *Emotional Intelligence: Why It Can Matter More Than IQ*. Bantam.

Griffin, T., & Amer. (2017, February 18). "12 Things About Product-Market Fit." *Andreessen Horowitz*. https://a16z.com/2017/02/18/12-things-about-product-market-fit-2/.

"Howard Schultz on Emotional Connections." (n.d.). Brand Autopsy. https://brandautopsy.typepad.com/brandautopsy/2005/06/howard_schultz_.html.

Klein, E. (2022, August 16). Opinion | "The Office Is Dying. It's Time to Rethink How We Work." *The New York Times*. https://www.nytimes.com/2022/08/16/opinion/ezra-klein-podcast-anne-helen-petersen-charlie-warzel.html.

management | Search Online Etymology Dictionary. (n.d.). https://www.etymonline.com/search?q=management.

Maslow, A. H. (2013). *A Theory of Human Motivation*. Simon and Schuster.

McGregor, D., & Cutcher-Gershenfeld, J. (2006). *The Human Side of Enterprise, Annotated Edition*. McGraw-Hill Professional.

Pascale, R. T. (1990) Managing on the Edge: How the Smartest Companies Use Conflict to Stay Ahead.

Sobel, R. (1999). *The Rise and Fall of the Conglomerate Kings*. Beard Books.

Stengel, J. (2012). *Grow: How Ideals Power Growth and Profit at the World's 50 Greatest Companies*. Random House.

Thompson, D. (2019, August 13). "The Religion of Workism Is Making Americans Miserable." *The Atlantic*. https://www.theatlantic.com/ideas/archive/2019/02/religion-workism-making-americans-miserable/583441/.

White, E. (2009, June 4). "Top CEOs Name Best Leadership Books." *WSJ*. https://www.wsj.com/articles/SB123178937550674293.

Chapter 3: What Individuals Want

"10 Classic Works of Medieval Literature Everyone Should Read." (2020, October 14). *Interesting Literature*. https://interestingliterature.com/2016/01/10-classic-works-of-medieval-literature-everyone-should-read/.

Adkins, B. J. H. a. A. (2023, April 19). "Employees Want a Lot More From Their Managers." Gallup.com. https://www.gallup.com/workplace/236570/employees-lot-managers.aspx.

Dishman, L. (2021, February 23). "Is now a good time to change careers? More workers are feeling good about it." *Fast Company*. https://www.fastcompany.com/90607167/is-now-a-good-time-to-change-careers-more-workers-are-feeling-good-about-it.

Ferriss, T. (2021). The Tim Ferriss Show Transcripts: "Safi Bahcall — On Hypnosis, Conquering Insomnia, Incentives, and More (#382)." *The Blog of Author Tim Ferriss*. https://tim.blog/2019/08/21/the-tim-ferriss-show-transcripts-safi-bahcall-on-hypnosis-conquering-insomnia-incentives-and-more-382/.

Gallup, Inc. (2023, April 3). *Gallup's Q12 Employee Engagement Survey - Gallup*. Gallup.com. https://www.gallup.com/workplace/356063/gallup-q12-employee-engagement-survey.aspx.

Goudreau, J. (2012, January 30). "So Begins A Quiet Revolution of the 50 Percent." *Forbes*. https://www.forbes.com/sites/jennagoudreau/2012/01/30/quiet-revolution-of-the-50-percent-introverts-susan-cain/?sh=bd487f893fb5.

Liu, J. (2019, October 31). "Nearly half of workers have made a dramatic career switch, and this is the average age they do it." CNBC. https://www.cnbc.com/2019/10/31/indeed-nearly-half-of-workers-have-made-a-dramatic-career-switch.html.

Marx, K., & Engels, F. (2009). *The Economic and Philosophic Manuscripts of 1844 and the Communist Manifesto.* Prometheus Books.

National Center for Education Statistics. (n.d.). Fast Facts: Undergraduate graduation rates (40). https://nces.ed.gov/fastfacts/display.asp?id=40.

Pew Research. "Americans' beliefs about the nature of God." (2022, April 15) Pew Research Center's Religion & Public Life Project. https://www.pewresearch.org/religion/2018/04/25/when-americans-say-they-believe-in-god-what-do-they-mean/.

purpose. https://dictionary.cambridge.org/dictionary/english/purpose#.

Staikos, B. (2022, September 29). "CX Organizational Structures That Work: Choose the Best Model for Your Business." Medallia | Customer Experience and Employee Experience. https://www.medallia.com/blog/cx-organizational-structures-that-work/.

Tabarrok, A. (2023, March 29). "The Law of Unintended Consequences—Marginal REVOLUTION." Marginal REVOLUTION. https://marginalrevolution.com/marginalrevolution/2023/03/the-law-of-unintended-consequences.html.

Taylor, C. (1992). *Sources of the Self: The Making of the Modern Identity.* Harvard University Press.

Team, E. (2018). "EdX Survey Finds that about 1/3 of Americans Ages 25 to 44 Have Completely Changed Fields Since Starting their First Job Post-College." *blog.edx.org.* https://blog.edx.org/edx-survey-finds-1-3-americans-ages-25-44-completely-changed-fields-since-starting-first-job-post-college.

"The Boss Factor: Making the world a better place through workplace relationships." (2020, September 22). McKinsey & Company. https://www.mckinsey.com/capabilities/people-and-organizational-performance/our-insights/the-boss-factor-making-the-world-a-better-place-through-workplace-relationships.

"The Kids Are Alright." Traceroute. (n.d.). https://traceroute.captivate.fm/episode/09-the-kids-are-alright.

Warren, R. (2003). *The Purpose-Driven Life: What on Earth Am I Here For?* Zondervan.

What is readability and why should content editors care about it? (2017, March 22). https://centerforplainlanguage.org/what-is-readability/#:~:text=The%20average%20American%20is%20considered,guidelines%20in%20the%20medical%20industry.

Chapter 4: What Companies Do

Beinhocker, E. D. (2006). "The Origin of Wealth: Evolution, Complexity, and the Radical Remaking of Economics." Harvard Business Press.

Von Clausewitz, C. (2008). *On War*. Princeton University Press.

Frankin, H. G. (1890). *PRINCIPLES OF ECONOMICS*. By Alfred Marshall, Professor of Political Economy in the University of Cambridge. MacMillan & Co., London and New York, 1890. Vol. I, pp. xxviii, 754. *Annals of the American Academy of Political and Social Science, 1*(2), 332–337. https://doi.org/10.1177/000271629000100217.

Friedman, M. (1970, September 13). "A Friedman doctrine—The Social Responsibility of Business Is to Increase Its Profits." *The New York Times*. https://www.nytimes.com/1970/09/13/archives/a-friedman-doctrine-the-social-responsibility-of-business-is-to.html.

Marshall, A. (1890). *Principles of Economics*.

Piketty, T. (2017). *Capital in the Twenty-First Century*. Harvard University Press.

"What is the productivity puzzle?" Office for National Statistics. (2015). *www.ons.gov.uk*. https://www.ons.gov.uk/employmentandlabourmarket/peopleinwork/labourproductivity/articles/whatistheproductivitypuzzle/2015-07-07.

"Why is Productivity Important?" *U.S. Bureau of Labor Statistics*. (2020, June 24). https://www.bls.gov/k12/productivity-101/content/why-is-productivity-important/home.htm#:~:text=With%20growth%20in%20productivity%2C%20an,as%20policymakers%20and%20government%20statisticians).

Chapter 5: What Companies Need

Coase, R. H. (1993). *The Nature of the Firm: Origins, Evolution, and Development.* Oxford University Press, USA.

Definition of Employee Engagement - Gartner Information Technology Glossary. (n.d.). Gartner. https://www.gartner.com/en/information-technology/glossary/employee-engagement.

Hundert, E. J., (1994). *The Enlightenment's Fable: Bernard Mandeville and the Discovery of Society.* Cambridge University Press.

Nadella, S. (2017). *Hit Refresh: A Memoir by Microsoft's CEO.* HarperCollins.

Scarry, R. (2010). *What Do People Do All Day?* HarperCollins.

Sharp, I. (2009). *Four Seasons: The Story of a Business Philosophy.* Penguin.

Smith, A. (2018). *The Theory of Moral Sentiments.* By Adam Smith, . . . The Second Edition. Gale Ecco, Print Editions.

The Sveriges Riksbank Prize in Economic Sciences in Memory of Alfred Nobel 1991. (n.d.). NobelPrize.org. https://www.nobelprize.org/prizes/economic-sciences/1991/coase/facts/.

Wikipedia contributors. (2023). Information economics. Wikipedia. https://en.wikipedia.org/wiki/Information_economics.

Chapter 6: What Employees Need

Baker, W.O. "The Paradox of Choice," *Symposium on Basic Research*, ed. Dael Wolfle, pp. 41-72. Washington, DC: American Association for the Advancement of Science, Publication No. 56 (1959).

Carson, R. (2002). *Silent Spring.* Houghton Mifflin Harcourt.

Celestine, N., PhD. (2023). "The Science of Happiness in Positive Psychology 101." *PositivePsychology.com.* https://positivepsychology.com/happiness/.

Chappell, T. (1993). *The Soul of a Business: Managing for Profit and the Common Good.* Bantam.

Editors of *Merriam-Webster*. (2022). "Sympathy vs. Empathy": What's the Difference? https://www.merriam-webster.com/words-at-play/sympathy-empathy-difference.

Evensky, J. (2015). *Adam Smith's Wealth of Nations: A Reader's Guide.* Cambridge University Press.

Greitemeyer, T., & Sagioglou, C. (2018). "The experience of deprivation: Does relative more than absolute status predict hostility?" *British Journal of Social Psychology, 58*(3), 515–533. https://doi.org/10.1111/bjso.12288.

Haidt, J. (2023, February 22). "Social Media is a Major Cause of the Mental Illness Epidemic in Teen Girls. Here's The Evidence." *Substack. After Babel.* https://jonathanhaidt.substack.com/p/social-media-mental-illness-epidemic.

Hayek, F. A. (2014). *The Road to Serfdom*: Text and Documents: The Definitive Edition. Routledge.

Hayek, F. A. (2017). *The Fatal Conceit: The Errors of Socialism*. Routledge.

"How to Be Successful, Learn about Tony Robbins. Key to Success." (2021, May 14). tonyrobbins.com. https://www.tonyrobbins.com/how-to-be-successful/#:~:text=Think%20about%20why%20you%20want,.%E2%80%9D%20That%27s%20a%20powerful%20purpose.

Liebenberg, L. (1990). *The Art of Tracking: The Origin of Science.* David Philip Publishers.

McDougall, C. (2009). *Born to Run: A Hidden Tribe, Superathletes, and the Greatest Race the World Has Never Seen.* Knopf.

Chapter 7: What Employees Must Do

Colvin, G. (2008) *Talent Is Overrated: What Really Separates World-Class Performers From Everybody Else.* Penguin Random House.

Dalio, R. (2018). *Principles.* Simon and Schuster.

Dweck, C. S. (2007). *Mindset: The New Psychology of Success.* Ballantine Books.

Jachimowicz, J. M. (2019, October 15). "3 reasons it's so hard to follow your passion." *Harvard Business Review*. https://hbr.org/2019/10/3-reasons-its-so-hard-to-follow-your-passion.

Kennedy, P. (2016) *Inventology: How We Dream Up Things That Change the World*. Mifflin Harcourt.

Magazine, S. (2018, April 29). "What's wrong with the lean startup methodology?" *Startup Mag*. Medium. *Medium*. https://medium.com/the-startup-magazine-collection/what-s-wrong-with-the-lean-startup-methodology-556ca2d5e30b.

Pagden, A., (1994) *European Encounters With the New World*. Yale University Press.

Pullman, P. (2002). *His Dark Materials: The Golden Compass (Book 1)*. Knopf Books for Young Readers.

Ries, E. (2011). "The Lean Startup: How Today's Entrepreneurs Use Continuous Innovation to Create Radically Successful Businesses." *Currency*.

Suzuki, S. (2020). *Zen Mind, Beginner's Mind*: 50th Anniversary Edition. Shambhala Publications.

Teets, C. (2012). *Golden Opportunity: Remarkable Careers That Began at McDonald's*. Cider Mill Press.

The Enneagram Institute. (n.d.). The Enneagram Institute. https://www.enneagraminstitute.com/.

The Myers & Briggs Foundation - MBTI® Basics. (n.d.). 2003-2023, the Myers and Briggs Foundation. https://www.myersbriggs.org/my-mbti-personality-type/mbti-basics/.

The Predictive Index. (2023, April 17). Talent Optimization Leader - The Predictive Index. https://www.predictiveindex.com/.

The Venn Diagram of Purpose. (2020, October 7). Ikigai Tribe. https://ikigaitribe.com/blogpost/the-venn-diagram-of-purpose/.

The Weight of Gold (2020) - IMDB. (2020, July 29). IMDb. https://www.imdb.com/title/tt8311394/.

"What is the DiSC assessment?" (n.d.). Discprofile.com. https://www.disc-profile.com/what-is-disc.

Wiseman, L. (2022, February 25). "Is Your Burnout From Too Much Work or Too Little Impact?" *Harvard Business Review*. https://hbr.org/2021/12/is-your-burnout-from-too-much-work-or-too-little-impact.

Chapter 8: What Managers Must Do

Adams, S. (1997). *The Dilbert Principle: A Cubicle's-Eye View of Bosses, Meetings, Management Fads & Other Workplace Afflictions*. Harper Collins.

Elberse, A. (2022, November 16). "Number One in Formula One." *Harvard Business Review*. https://hbr.org/2022/11/number-one-in-formula-one.

Humphrey, W. S. (1988). "Characterizing the software process: a maturity framework." *IEEE Software*, 5(2), 73–79. https://doi.org/10.1109/52.2014.

Klatt, B., Murphy, S., Irvine, D. (2003), "Accountability: Getting a Grip on Results."

"Netflix Culture Freedom and Responsibility." (n.d.). Scribd. https://www.scribd.com/document/565391550/Netflix-Culture-Freedom-and-Responsibility.

Chapter 9: WHY's Golden Future

"2017 Cone Communications CSR Study." (2017, December 18). https://engageforgood.com/2017-cone-communications-csr-study/.

Anantavarasilpa, C. (2023). "Happiness and Productivity: With happier workers, business thrives." Smiles at Work | the Official Happily Blog. https://blog.happily.ai/happiness-and-productivity-with-happier-workers-business-thrives/.

Babiak, P., & Hare, R. D. (2009). *Snakes in Suits: When Psychopaths Go to Work*. Harper Collins.

'CareerBuilder Hiring Solutions. (2011, March 28). More Than One-Quarter of Managers Said They Weren't Ready to Lead When They Began Managing Others, Finds New CareerBuilder Survey...' Press Room | Career Builder. https://press.careerbuilder.com/2011-03-28-More-Than-One-Quarter-of-

Managers-Said-They-Werent-Ready-to-Lead-When-They-Began-Manag-ing-Others-Finds-New-CareerBuilder-Survey.

Crossover. (n.d.). *Crossover.* https://www.crossover.com/perspective/remote-work-is-here-to-stay-what-to-do-now.

De Saint Pierre, C. I. C. (1767). *A Project for Perpetual Peace.* by J. J. Rousseau or rather, abridged by him from the "Projet de paix perpétuelle" of the Abbé de Saint Pierre. Translated from the French by Thomas Nugent, with a preface by the translator.

De Secondat, Baron De Montesquieu, C. (1950). *Oeuvres complètes de Montesquieu: Pensées.* Spicilège. Geographica. Voyages.

Discussion paper 17: "Are Sweatshops Profit-Maximizing?" *Better Work.* (2023, April 21). Better Work. https://betterwork.org/reports-and-publi-cations/better-work-discussion-paper-n17/.

Elite Rides, #MotivationalMonday &qout;Profit is the reward. . . (n.d.). https://m.facebook.com/eliterides.org/photos/a.2537108119890581/2872902892977767/?locale=hi_IN.

Empathy Quotient (EQ). (2004). Psychology Tools. https://psychology-tools.com/test/empathy-quotient.

Environmental, Social and Governance Summary Report FY 2022. (2023). Walmart. https://corporate.walmart.com/esgreport/media-library/docu-ment/walmart-fy2022-esg-summary/_proxyDocument?id=00000182-21ec-d591-afe2-2bfcb4df0000.

FRB Speech, Greenspan, Productivity, October 23, 2002. (n.d.). https://www.federalreserve.gov/boarddocs/speeches/2002/20021023/default.htm.*Generative AI Could Raise Global GDP by 7%.* (n.d.). Goldman Sachs. https://www.goldmansachs.com/intelligence/pages/generative-ai-could-raise-global-gdp-by-7-percent.html.

Graeber, D. (2019). *Bullshit Jobs: A Theory.* Simon & Schuster.

Harter, B. J. (2023, April 5). "Employee Engagement on the Rise in the U.S." *Gallup.com.* https://news.gallup.com/poll/241649/employee-engage-ment-rise.aspx.

Harter, B. R. J. B. a. J. (2023, April 19). "Why Great Managers Are So Rare" *Gallup.com*. https://www.gallup.com/workplace/231593/why-great-managers-rare.aspx.

Kadlec, C. W. (1999). *Dow 100,000: Fact or Fiction.*

Keynes, J. M. (1987). *Economic Possibilities for Our Grandchildren.*

Kolmar, C. (2023). 20+ Essential Part-Time Job Statistics [2023]: Who Works Part-Time And Why? Zippia. https://www.zippia.com/advice.part-time-job-statistics/#:~:text=In%20more%20detail%2C%20 63.1%25%20of,million%20employed%20full%2Dtime%20workers.

McKee, R. (1997) *Story: Substance, Structure, Style and the Principles of Screenwriting*. Regan Books.

Muro, M., Maxim, R., & Whiton, J. (2022, March 9). "Automation and Artificial Intelligence: How machines are affecting people and places." *Brookings*. https://www.brookings.edu/research/automation-and-artificial-intelligence-how-machines-affect-people-and-places/.

NielsenIQ. (2021, February 17). "Doing well by doing good, "NIQ. https://nielseniq.com/global/en/insights/report/2014/doing-well-by-doing-good/.

Philip-Lye, C. (2023, January 4). "Startup employees happier than tech giant workers, survey finds." *APOLLO Insurance*. APOLLO Insurance. https://apollocover.com/magazine/startup-employees-happier-than-tech-giant-workers-survey-finds/.

Pink, D. H. (2006). *A Whole New Mind: Why Right-Brainers Will Rule the Future*. Penguin.

Ropek, L. (2023, May 17). "10 Signs That the AI "Revolution" Is Spinning Out of Control." Gizmodo. https://gizmodo.com/ai-chatgpt-bing-google-8-sign-revolution-out-of-control-1850076241.

Roy, N. (2022, October 7). "Four-day working week pros and cons as a third of Scots businesses plan for it." *Daily Record*. https://www.dailyrecord.co.uk/lifestyle/four-day-working-week-pros-28180415.

Schor, J. (n.d.). *The case for a 4-day work week* [Video]. TED Talks. https://www.ted.com/talks/juliet_schor_the_case_for_a_4_day_work_week/transcript.

Seidman, D. (2011). *How: Why How We Do Anything Means Everything*. John Wiley & Sons.

SHRM (2020, August 12). "Survey: 84 Percent of U.S. Workers Blame Bad Managers for Creating Unnecessary Stress." *SHRM*. https://www.shrm. org/about-shrm/press-room/press-releases/pages/survey-84-percent-of-us-workers-blame-bad-managers-for-creating-unnecessary-stress-.aspx.

"Solving the productivity puzzle." (2018, February 20). McKinsey & Company. https://www.mckinsey.com/featured-insights/regions-in-focus/solving-the-productivity-puzzle.

Suzuki, D. (2011). *Essays in Zen Buddhism*. Souvenir Press.

Table B-2. Average weekly hours and overtime of all employees on private nonfarm payrolls by industry sector, seasonally adjusted - 2023 M05 Results. (n.d.). https://www.bls.gov/news.release/empsit.t18.htm.

"The Deloitte Global 2023 Gen Z and Millennial Survey." (2023, May 17). Deloitte. https://www.deloitte.com/global/en/issues/work/content/genz-millennialsurvey.html.

"The Potentially Large Effects of Artificial Intelligence on Economic Growth" (Briggs/Kodnani). (2023, March 27). GS Research. https://www.gspublishing.com/content/research/en/reports/2023/03/27/d64e052b-0f6e-45d7-967b-d7be35fabd16.html.

"The Productivity–Pay Gap." (n.d.). Economic Policy Institute. https://www.epi.org/productivity-pay-gap/.

Twaronite, K. (2021, August 31). "A Global Survey on the Ambiguous State of Employee Trust." *Harvard Business Review*. https://hbr.org/2016/07/a-global-survey-on-the-ambiguous-state-of-employee-trust.

Vardi, N. (2018, November 19). "How A Mysterious Tech Billionaire Created Two Fortunes—And A Global Software Sweatshop." *Forbes*. https://www.forbes.com/sites/nathanvardi/2018/11/19/how-a-mysterious-tech-billionaire-created-two-fortunesand-a-global-software-sweatshop/?sh=17008e966cff.

Why is Generation Z deemed to be the lost generation? (n.d.). Quora. https://www.quora.com/Why-is-the-Generation-Z-deemed-to-be-the-lost-generation.

Wikipedia contributors. (2023). Working time. Wikipedia. https://en.wikipedia.org/wiki/Working_time#cite_note-bls-employment-66.

Work, G. P. T. (n.d.). "Walmart Inc." Great Place to Work. https://www.greatplacetowork.com/certified-company/1120506.

About the Authors

STEPHEN BUTLER is a management consultant, entrepreneur and keynote speaker. He worked as a capital and commodity markets development executive and startup/tech CEO before becoming a founding member of BDC's Growth Driver Program for High Impact Firms, and Framework, an advisory network. His talk, "Why Your Job Isn't Meaningless," was featured globally by TEDx in 2024. Stephen holds a PhD in Social and Political Sciences (Cambridge), a BA (Hons) in Economics and Political Science (McGill), and taught at Harvard as a Visiting Fellow. He lives in Calgary and San Francisco.

KARISSA PRICE is Chief Marketing Officer at Dragonfruit AI. She has worked as a Fortune 100 marketing executive, including Walmart's VP Marketing, Food, Consumables and Health & Wellness, has run two health care companies, and has consulted widely. She holds a PhD in International Political Economy (Harvard) and a BA (cum laude) in Political Science and Government (UC San Diego). She lives in Sun Valley.

They began their business careers together at The Boston Consulting Group and cofounded Sagely, a consultancy.

NOTE FROM THE AUTHORS

If you've enjoyed *Why Is a Verb*, we invite you to help others discover it by leaving a review and sharing on your preferred platform.

For our most recent thoughts—and to join the conversation—please visit www.sagely.ltd.

www.ingramcontent.com/pod-product-compliance
Lightning Source LLC
Chambersburg PA
CBHW031847200326
41597CB00012B/298